Creative China Painting

*To my sons, Roger and Ashley,
and my friend, Julia Osorno*

CREATIVE CHINA PAINTING

WANDA SUTTON

SEARCH PRESS

Wanda Sutton studied architecture before embarking on a three-year ceramic course at Nottingham College of Art. She went on to teach ceramics, general painting and design in Germany and Belgium. This was followed by three years in Singapore where she taught art and crafts and studied Chinese brush painting. Many of Wanda's underwater designs were inspired by time spent scuba diving off Eastern Malaya and cataloguing shells and coral.

Wanda has taught ceramics, sculpture, Chinese brushwork and painting on china for over two decades at Bracknell College of Further Education, in Berkshire. Her work has been frequently exhibited, and she has held seminars on china painting throughout the South of England.

Wanda lives in Sandhurst, Berkshire.

First published in Great Britain 1998

Search Press Limited
Wellwood, North Farm Road,
Tunbridge Wells, Kent TN2 3DR

Photographs by Search Press Studios

ISBN 0 85532 874 6

With thanks to Pam Philip, June Williams, Sophie Williams and Mac Collingwood for lending items featured in this book.

With thanks also to Roger for typing the original manuscript.

Publishers' note

All the step-by-step photographs in this book show the author, Wanda Sutton, demonstrating how to paint on china. No models have been used.

It is the publishers' custom to recommend synthetic materials as substitutes for animal products wherever possible. For most purposes, brushes made from artificial fibres are just as satisfactory as those made from natural fibres. However, it should be pointed out that for some china painting techniques, natural-haired brushes will produce softer effects.

If you have any difficulty in obtaining any of the materials and equipment mentioned in this book, then please write to the publishers for a current list of stockists, which includes firms who operate a mail-order service.

If you are interested in any other art and craft books published by Search Press, please send for a free catalogue to:

SEARCH PRESS LTD.,
Department B, Wellwood, North Farm Road, Tunbridge Wells, Kent TN2 3DR
Tel. (01892) 510850 Fax (01892) 515903
E-mail: sales@searchpress.com

or (if resident in the USA) to:
ARTHUR SCHWARTZ & CO., INC.,
234 Meads Mountain Road, Woodstock, NY 12498
Tel: (914) 679 4024 Fax: (914) 679 4093
Orders: Toll-free 800 669 9080

Colour separation by P&W Graphics, Singapore
Printed in Spain by Elkar S. Coop. Bilbao 48012

Lace hydrangeas on an earthenware tile
A medium square shader was used to paint blue, pink and
turquoise petals, then a dotted effect in between clusters was
created using a wipe-out tool. Green leaves were painted in
and the tile was fired at 800ºC (1475ºF).

Contents

Introduction

Painting on china is a fascinating and absorbing pastime. It is amazing how many different decorative effects can be created – my designs range from the traditional to the contemporary, and incorporate many different subjects. After you have learnt the basic techniques, you too will find that the possibilities are endless. This book will guide you through mixing and creating colours, and applying paints, reliefs, lustres and gold. I hope that you will then be able to create your own original patterns and pictures and will be inspired by the beauty of the fired designs.

The materials required for painting on china are relatively inexpensive. If you are initially learning only the basic skills, you do not have to buy all the colours or all the brushes – be selective and purchase a small range of materials to begin with. The biggest outlay is a kiln so, if you are learning to paint on china, it is worth contacting a local college or school to enquire whether you could have access to a kiln, or to join a class until you are sure whether or not you want to continue with the craft.

The best china to paint on is white bone china, porcelain, or plain white earthenware tiles. Good seconds can be bought from specialist suppliers. This type of china is already glazed and can be hand painted. The finished item is then fired to 'fix' the decorated surface. Plates, bowls, dishes, teapots, jugs, boxes, plaques and jewellery blanks can be all be painted and transformed to match existing china, or to fit in with your decor. I hope that anyone interested in the decorative arts will find this book a good source of design and will be inspired by the variety of painting styles within these pages.

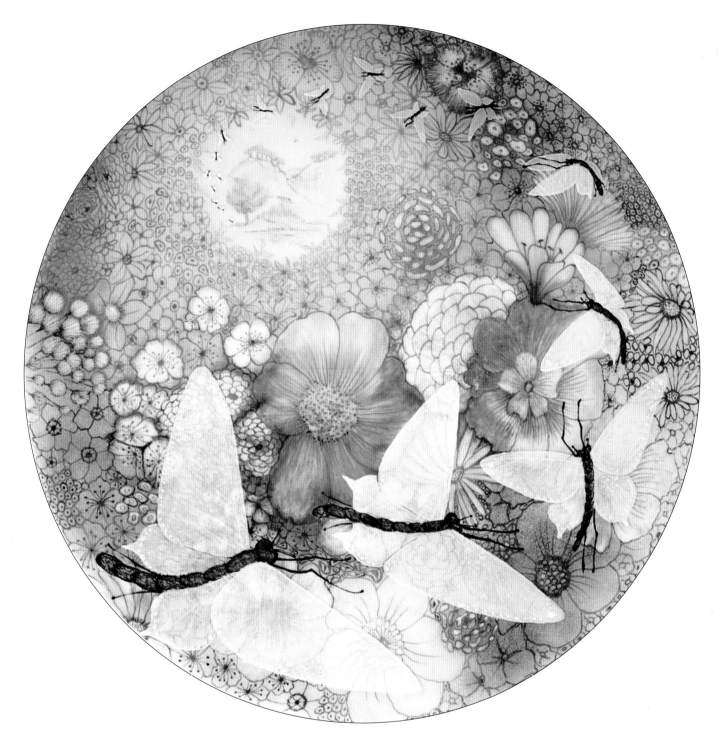

Butterflies on a porcelain tile
Relief enamel butterflies were applied over a painted background embellished with fine penwork. First, soft shades were painted over the surface and blended into each other with a cosmetic sponge. Dots of turpentine were dropped in to form flower heads, and petals were wiped out. The tile was then fired at 820ºC (1510ºF). Large and small flower heads were drawn in and a small scene was painted in over the lightest area. The tile was fired again at 810ºC (1490ºF). The butterflies were drawn on to tracing paper, cut out and arranged on the tile in an attractive pattern. They were then traced on to the painted surface and a thin, translucent coat of relief enamel was applied to each one. The tile was fired at 800ºC (1475ºF).

Materials

You do not have to buy all the materials shown in this book to start painting on china, although you will have to have access to a kiln (see pages 92–93). You can start off with just a paintbrush, some paints and a plain white tile.

PAINTS

On-glaze paints are available in many different colours, and in powder form in small pots or packets. These metal oxide colourings are only available from china painting suppliers and they are specially formulated for painting on glazed porcelain or bone china.

There are different makes of paint available, so you will have to experiment with each of the manufacturers' products and keep notes as you develop your preferences.

You can work with a limited palette to start off with. I use the range of colours shown below, together with white, which I use for lightening shades. Highlights are created by wiping areas of paint away to reveal the white china beneath.

The colours shown can be mixed to create a much wider range, but if you decide to extend your palette, avoid mixing cadmium- or selenium-based reds and oranges with iron reds, as they will burn away.

yellow

light blue

yellow ochre

dark blue

iron red

blue-green

mid-brown

mid-green

black

deep pink

> **NOTE**
> Paint manufacturers have different names for the same colour so it is not possible to give specific names. You will gradually learn from experience which suits you best.

These basic colours can be mixed together to produce an extensive palette. White may be used to lighten shades. It is advisable to test colours before using them, as the colours sometimes alter after firing. Mix different shades – light, medium and dark – then place them in sequence on a tile, and reference each colour. Fire the colours at 800ºC (1475ºF) and keep the tile as a firing guide.

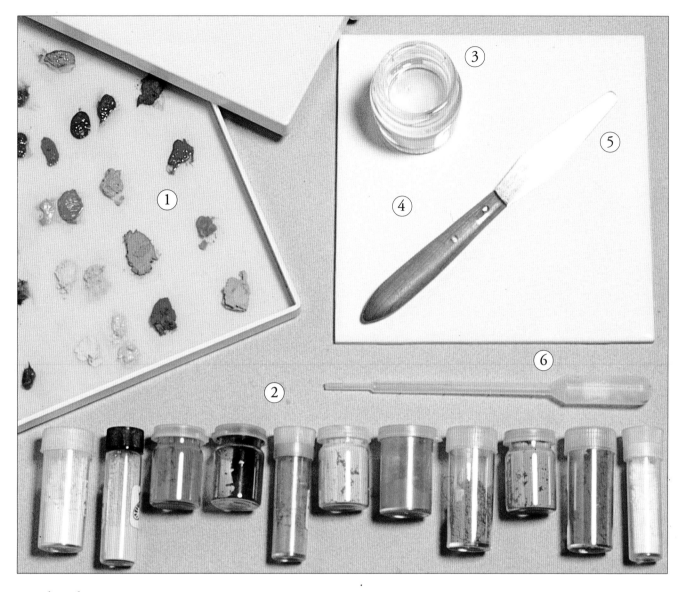

1. Palette box

An airtight box to hold the mixed paints

2. Powder paints

These can only be obtained from china painting suppliers. They are available in an enormous range of colours, but the basic colours needed are shown on page 8. From this basic palette, almost any colour imaginable can be created.

3. Open medium

This is also referred to as non-drying or slow-drying medium. It is an oil that is mixed with the powder colour. A water-based medium is available if you are allergic to turpentine.

4. White tile

For grinding and mixing colours on.

5. Palette knife

For mixing the paint.

6. Pipette

For picking up drops of oil or water.

1. Large square shader

Used for large background areas such as skies or seas, and for large flower petals and leaves. The square shader is also known as a flat brush.

2. Medium square shader

Used for a variety of paintwork. Use a synthetic brush for groundlay work, using resist, lustre work and painting with gold. Use a separate brush for each medium.

3. Small square shader

Used for small flowers, birds and animals, filling in bodies, or painting petals or wings.

4. Medium round brush

Used for small flower petals, leaves, buds, berries, distant birds and figures.

5. Small pointer brush

Used for fine gold lines, dots, scrolls, eyes and details such as insect legs. It can also be used for platinum. Keep one brush for use with gold and one for platinum.

6. Small scroller brush

Used for long sweeping lines, detail and for laying relief enamel in scrolls.

7. Blender brush

Used for gently wafting over the painted work to blend one colour into another leaving no hard lines.

NOTE

Always choose good quality, soft-haired brushes, and keep synthetic ones exclusively for groundlay work, painting with gold, using resists and lustrework.

Always clean your brushes thoroughly when you have finished painting. Paints are cleaned using turpentine or the cleaner recommended by the supplier; groundlay oil (see page 72) is cleaned off with turpentine; resist is cleaned off with warm water and soap; lustre is cleaned off with lustre thinner; and gold is cleaned off with lustre thinner or lavender oil. Dry brushes well with a tissue, and dip them into olive oil or baby oil to keep them from becoming brittle. Wipe off the excess oil and smooth the tips into shape with a cloth before storing them in an upright container. If you look after your brushes in this way, they should last a long time.

---

8. Peelable resist

Used to mask off areas when painting. Always use a synthetic brush with the resist and clean it thoroughly after use with soap and warm water.

9. Cotton wool

This is used under a square of silk when groundlaying and softening painted areas, or over a cocktail stick or toothpick when cleaning.

10. Fine cosmetic sponge

This is used for many things, including to soften paintwork and to apply paint or lustres.

11. Square of silk, sponge and elastic band

Silk is secured over a piece of sponge or cotton wool with an elastic band and used to prepare the groundlay or to soften a painted area.

12. Cocktail sticks or toothpicks

You can place a little cotton wool over the tip of a cocktail stick or toothpick and use this for cleaning.

13. Chinagraph pencil

For drawing the design on to china.

14. Wipe-out tool

A double-ended rubber tool used to take off paint to create dots, fine lines and highlights.

15. Lint-free cloth

Brushes loaded with medium should be pressed on to a small square of lint-free cloth to prepare them for painting.

16. Tissues

For cleaning china and brushes and for general mopping up.

17. Methylated spirit

This is used to clean the china before it is painted.

18. Pure turpentine

This is used for cleaning brushes. There is also a cleaner available from specialist suppliers that can be used in place of turpentine if you are allergic to it. Alternatively, use the brush cleaner recommended by the manufacturer of the paints you are using. Do not use white spirit.

CHINA

Plain, white glazed china is ideal for china painting, and should be used for all the projects shown in this book unless otherwise specified. The shape of the item is an important part of the design, so think about this when purchasing plates, cups and so on. Traditional shapes lend themselves to traditional designs – although it can be challenging to create contemporary patterns on traditional teapots, plaques or bowls.

It is wise to learn about what you are painting on before you begin. Bone china (antimony, or tin plus bone) and porcelain (china clay) are made up of different materials. Bone china contains clay mixed with up to fifty per cent of finely ground bone. It is this mixture that gives bone china its luminous translucency – your hand can be seen behind a plate if you hold it up to the light. Bone china is also shinier than porcelain and it has a softer glaze, so any paints that are applied over the glaze sink into the surface, and fix in the kiln at a lower temperature. Porcelain has a harder glaze and the pieces have a slightly grey-white look when compared with bone china. Paint should not be applied on to porcelain too thickly, as it may chip off or stand proud of the surface.

You can also paint on earthenware tiles. These are available in white, cream or brick red. They are a coarser china, but they are inexpensive and very easy to work on.

A selection of plain, white, glazed china suitable for painting.

Starting to paint

Your workplace should be comfortable, well-lit and dust-free. Allow yourself enough room to work, so that you have easy access to your paints. I work on a table covered with clean paper or card. As I am right-handed, I have the light directed from the left-hand side on to my work.

The powdered paints are mixed with a medium before starting to paint. There are two types available – an open non-drying oil medium (also called a non-drying or slow-drying medium) which allows you more time to work on your painting and design, or a quick-drying medium. With an open medium, the depth of colour is achieved by building up thin coats on top of each other, and firing in between each application. The open medium is easier to use, but colours can be accidentally smudged if you are not careful. The following sequence shows how to mix the paint with open medium.

MIXING THE PAINT

1. The china must be absolutely clean before starting to paint. Rub all the surfaces thoroughly using a tissue dipped in methylated spirit, then dry the china thoroughly.

2. Place a little powder paint on to a clean tile.

3. Use a pipette to transfer open medium to the paint. Place a little extra medium on to the tile.

4. Grind the mixture well and work it up into a small neat lump. The mixture should be the consistency of toothpaste. If it is too runny, add a tiny amount of powder paint; if it is too dry, add a drop of open medium.

5. Mixed paint must be kept clean and dust-free. Any paint that is not required for immediate use can be referenced and transferred to an air-tight palette box using the tip of a palette knife. It can then be stored for later use.

> *NOTE*
> The pink or purple ranges can be very gritty, so if you are preparing any of these, make sure that they are really well ground.

BRUSHWORK

There are many different painting techniques, ranging from simple brush strokes to more elaborate applications of colour and texture. In this section I show how to create pictures, patterns and motifs using powder colour mixed with open medium.

Brushing is the application and spreading of colour over the painting surface using a variety of different sized paint brushes. The best way to start painting is to practise brush strokes with different brushes on plain white tiles. This will soon help you to build up your confidence and skills.

Place a small prepared amount of colour (see page 13) on to a clean tile using a palette knife. It is essential that you choose the correct sized brushes for the strokes you want to make and it is advisable to work with fairly dry brushes. To start, use a small pointer; dip it into the medium then press it on to a spare clean tile to remove any excess oil. Gently press the brush down on to a clean piece of lint-free cloth to prepare it for painting. Now carefully work it into the paint. Practise using the brush, lifting, pressing and pulling a variety of shapes on the tile. Do not overwork the strokes – keep them clean and well-defined. If the paint drags and misses areas, it is too dry and you will have to add a drop more medium. If the paint has a shiny appearance, or even stands up a little from the surface, it is too oily and is being applied too thickly. Add a little more powder paint to the mixture.

Always rinse your brushes in turpentine or the cleaner recommended by the supplier, and wipe them before reloading them for the next strokes.

NOTE
To avoid spoiling the tip of your brush, work it into the paint and gently draw it through the colour.

You can create a variety of strokes by varying the angle of the brush. Practise using more pressure and less pressure, and painting straight strokes and curved strokes to achieve different tones.

A small pointer brush can be used to create thin strokes.

Brush strokes can be worked into each other to create leaves and foliage.

The edge of a square shader can be used to create thin and thick lines.

A square shader can be worked across the tile in one stroke to create a dark to light shaded finish. The brush should be worked into the right-hand side of the paint, using a circular anticlockwise movement to pick up more paint on the left side of the brush.

A square shader can be used to create curved strokes.

A square shader can be used to create petals and leaves.

NOTE

Do not rework strokes. If you make a mistake, or if you do not like the design or colours you have used, wipe the paint off the china surface and start again.

PAINTING FLOWERS AND LEAVES ~ *Hibiscus*

Using the strokes you have just practised you can paint your first flower. In this demonstration, I have used just one colour, but once you have practised the technique, you can introduce more colours into your flowers and add further detail. Before starting to paint, practise drawing the design on paper.

Keep a sketch book and record your ideas. Refer to your test palette (see page 8) before choosing which colours you would like to use. Sketch directly on to the china using a chinagraph pencil. If you do not feel confident about drawing without a guide, you can transfer the sketch on to the surface of the china using tracing paper. To do this, place tracing paper on top of the design. Trace the design using a sharp pencil or ball point pen. Attach the tracing to the china using two small pieces of masking tape. Slide a piece of black or red carbon paper underneath and draw over the lines. The design should now be transferred on to the china and it is ready to paint. The black or red carbon lines will burn away in the kiln.

YOU WILL NEED
YOU WILL NEED
Chinagraph pencil
Medium square shader
Small pointer brush
Small scroller brush
Powder paint: blue
Open medium

1. Sketch the design of the hibiscus using a chinagraph pencil. The sketched lines will burn off in the kiln.

2. Use a medium square shader to paint in the petals. Lay in the petals at the back of the flower first.

3. Continue building up the petals until the flower is complete.

4. Add the bud using a small pointer brush. Be careful not to smudge the flower as you work.

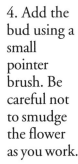

5. Paint in the branches using a small pointer brush. Pull the paint down towards the bottom of the image to create an impression of light and shade.

6. Add the pistil using a small scroller brush. Work from the centre of the flower to the tip. Add the stamen.

TOP LEFT
Garrya elliptica *The flowers were painted with a medium round brush using dotted lines. The leaves were added with a small square shader, using a deeper shade on the left side of the brush.*

TOP RIGHT
Plum blossom *A medium round brush and a circular stroke were used to paint in each petal. Sepals and leaves were added using the same brush, and stamens were then worked with a small pointer brush.*

MIDDLE
Chinese butterfly *The body was painted with one stroke of a medium round brush. Wings were added using two strokes of a small square shader. Details such as the legs, antennae and head, were worked with a small pointer brush.*

BOTTOM RIGHT
Chinese wild orchid *The leaves were painted with a small scroller brush, and the stem and flower were added using a small pointer brush. The flower was painted using one single stroke for each petal, working from the centre of the growing point in the Chinese style.*

BOTTOM LEFT
Hibiscus *The step-by-step sequence opposite shows how to paint this flower.*

PAINTING FEATHERS ~ *Pheasant*

Feathers were used as a source of design in the early nineteenth century by one of the Worcester potteries, and these designs are now much sought after by collectors. They were painted in a realistic style, usually on the rim of a plate, saucer or cup. The edges of the items were then painted with gilt bands, and occasionally small stylised flowers were added as a finishing touch.

I collect as many feathers as I can whilst out walking, and I then sketch out my designs using them as reference. Arrange the feathers in different patterns on a piece of white paper. You can use lots of feathers – grouped, arranged vertically or horizontally, or joined up to give a patchwork effect – but a single image can be just as effective.

> *YOU WILL NEED*
> Chinagraph pencil
> Small square shader
> Powder paints: green, brown, black and pale grey
> Open medium
> Blender brush
> Wipe-out tool
> Medium square shader

1. Use a chinagraph pencil to draw the design lightly on to the surface of the china. Paint in the design using a small square shader and brown mixed with black and a touch of green. Gently waft a blender brush over the colours to soften the lines.

2. Pull a wipe-out tool down the centre to represent the quill. Work from the top of the feather down.

3. Use a medium square shader to gently lay in a thin coat of pale grey to create a delicate effect. Pull the colour out from the centre.

4. Use the wipe-out tool to wipe away the quill. Stroke over the colours with a soft, dry medium square shader. Use a curved or wavy stroke to move the paint around the design.

> *NOTE*
> Do not use a fine pointed brush when painting feathers as this will produce a harsher and less subtle result.

Bone china trinket box and porcelain plate
Both these items use the technique shown opposite to create a feather design. You can see how realistic the painting is by comparing the painted feathers around the border of the plate with the real ones placed in the centre of it.

Porcelain vases
Peacock feathers often have an iridescent sheen. This can be achieved by painting turquoise or bronze green on to the design. The work can then be fired at 820°C (1510°F) if porcelain or 780°C (1435°F) if bone china. If you are painting a black feather, first paint it in with deep blue or green. Fire it, then apply black over the top and re-fire. Black on its own can look very flat.

19

PAINTING AGATES ~ *Onyx*

You can work freely and imaginatively with this decorating technique, and even a nervous painter will be able to create beautiful work easily. My inspiration is drawn from my travels. I have collected many pebbles, cut agates, onyx and petrified chips of wood over the years. The lovely colours and patterns can be painted on to china easily, but to achieve a good depth, two to four firings are required.

You can decorate china with borders, bands and edges, panels of colour or all-over patterns, or you can combine them with oriental designs, and stylised or realistic painting. Just apply the colour following the step-by-step instructions below.

Onyx textures vary greatly, so you do not have to copy patterns exactly.

YOU WILL NEED
Powder paints: yellow-green, olive green, sepia, golden brown, dark brown and iron red
Open medium
Medium square shader
Small scroller brush
Blender brush
Turpentine
Tissue

1. Prepare the colours in your palette and work from light to dark. Lay in yellow-green over some areas using a medium square shader.

2. Use the same brush to shade in olive green. Blend in the colours as you work.

3. Clean your brush and softly cover areas with sepia and golden brown. Waft over the colours with a blender brush to soften any hard lines.

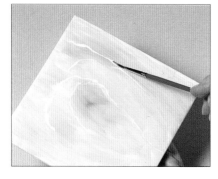

4. Take a small scroller brush and dip it in turpentine. Wipe it on a tissue and draw the brush, with a slight wiggle, up and down the surface, turning it as you work to add interest and shape. If you are working on porcelain, fire at 820°C (1510°F), or 780°C (1435°F) if using bone china.

5. Use olive green, dark brown and iron red and apply them thinly using a medium square shader. The design is now ready for the second firing, which should be done at the same temperature as the first firing.

6. Paint your design all over with a very thin coat of olive green. Fire it at 810°C (1490°F) if porcelain, or 770°C (1420°F) if bone china.

Onyx on bone china bowl

The four white panels inside the bowl were masked off with masking tape. The first onyx colours were painted on to the remaining areas inside and out (see opposite), and the masking tape was removed. The bowl was then fired at 780ºC (1435ºF). Using the same onyx colours, stylised designs were painted on the white panels, and more colour was applied to the remaining inside coloured panels. The bowl was then fired at 780ºC (1435ºF). A second coat was then applied to the outside to strengthen the colours, and the bowl was fired at 770ºC (1420ºF). The final application of colours was applied to the inside panels and the outside, and the bowl was fired at 770ºC (1420ºF). Finally, the outlines and details were highlighted using a pen and burnished gold. A brush was used to edge the rim with gold. The bowl was fired at 760ºC (1400ºF).

Green onyx porcelain vase

This was painted in the same manner as the tile shown opposite. It was fired initially at 820ºC (1510ºF), and then at 810ºC (1490ºF).

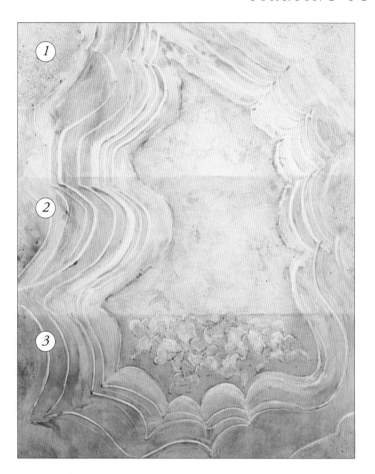

Lace agate

1. Bands of pale blue, ivory and flesh were painted against central bands of grey using a square shader. The grey areas were textured, and given a lace-like appearance by wiping away small areas of paint using a fine scroller brush which had been dipped in turpentine then dried until just damp. The surface was then softened with a dry crumpled tissue. The tile was fired at 800ºC (1475ºF).

2. Pale blue-grey was applied to deepen areas of colour and a few lines were wiped out. The tile was fired at 800ºC (1475ºF).

3. A thin coat of pale pink-grey was painted all over and the lace area was sponged. Some lines and the centre lace were wiped out. The tile was fired at 800ºC (1475ºF).

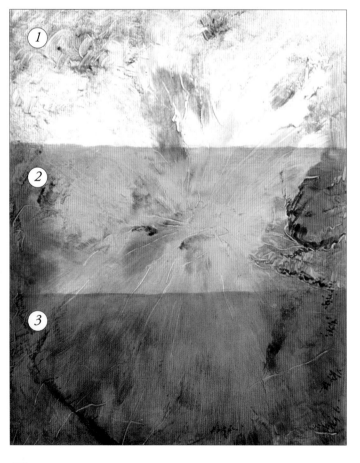

Petrified rainbow wood agate

1. Blocks and lines of iron red, pale blue, sepia and yellow were applied and then softened with a square shader. The tile was fired at 800ºC (1475ºF).

2. More blue, iron red and yellow-green were added. Textured areas were wiped out and the tile was then fired at 800ºC (1475ºF).

3. Iron red was painted thinly all over and a touch of violet was added. The tile was fired at 800ºC (1475ºF).

Brown agate

1. *Areas of yellow, golden brown and mid-brown were painted using a square shader. Agate bands were created with a wipe-out tool (see page 26), but you could drag the serrated edge of a piece of thin card over the tile to create bands of colour. The tile was then fired at 800ºC (1475ºF).*

2. *The colours were built up with iron red, chestnut and sepia. Selected areas were wiped out with a wipe-out tool and the tile was fired at 800ºC (1475ºF).*

3. *A thin coat of dark brown was painted all over the surface and texture was added to some areas using a crumpled tissue. The tile was fired at 800ºC (1475ºF).*

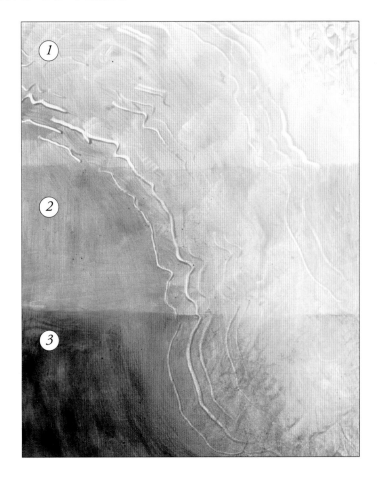

Labradorite agate

1. *Light turquoise, pale blue, dark blue and orange were worked into waves using a square shader. Details were then added using yellow ochre. The tile was fired at 800ºC (1475ºF).*

2. *Deeper blue-green and violet were painted into the waves. The tile was fired at 800ºC (1475ºF).*

3. *Finally, dark blue was painted thinly over the whole surface. The tile was fired at 800ºC (1475ºF).*

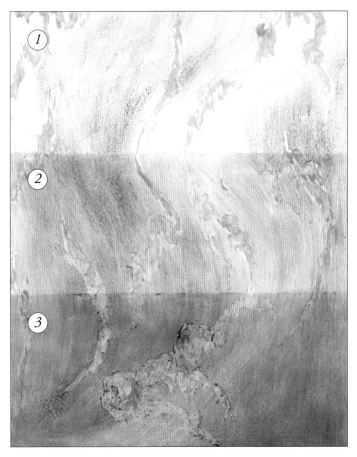

Butterflies on a bone china trinket box
This is a variation on petrified wood agate, showing a more pronounced wood texture. A circle was lightly sketched on to the lid. Yellow ochre, mid-brown and dark brown were applied. The box was fired at 780ºC (1435ºF). The three butterflies were sketched in and then painted. Mid-brown and a touch of black were painted thinly in bands over the base coat. The box was fired at 770ºC (1420ºF). A thin coat of iron red was painted all over the background, allowing the textures to show through. The box was fired at 770ºC (1420ºF). Finally, the gold design was applied in liquid bright gold and the box was fired at 760ºC (1400ºF).

Labradorite agate on a bone china trinket box
A circle was sketched on to the lid and, then the colours were applied (see pages 20 and 23). The box was fired at 780ºC (1435ºF). A small posy of stylised flowers was painted in the central area of the lid, and a second labradorite coat applied. Relief enamel dots were then added and the box was fired at 770ºC (1420ºF). The relief enamel dots were then gilded with liquid bright gold and a third labradorite coat was added. The box was fired at 760ºC (1400ºF).

OPPOSITE

Malachite and hibiscus on a bone china lamp base
Yellow-green, olive green and sepia were softly painted on in certain areas of the lamp base. It was fired at 780ºC (1435ºF). The grain and texture were painted with the same colours, together with black. A wipe-out tool was used to form waves and swirls. It was fired at 770ºC (1420ºF). Emerald green was painted thinly all over to allow the coat beneath to shine through, and it was fired at 770ºC (1420ºF).

Red agate and cherry blossom on a bone china lamp base
Areas of iron red, pale blue and deep grey were painted over the panels, base and top, then the lamp was fired at 780ºC (1435ºF). The cherry blossom design was sketched then painted on to the white panels, then a second thin coat of grey paint was applied to deepen the dark grey areas. It was fired at 770ºC (1420ºF). A thin coat of iron red was applied, and it was fired again at 770ºC (1420ºF). Finally, gold lines were added and the cherry blossom was outlined using liquid bright gold. The lamp base was fired at 760ºC (1400ºF).

Wiping out

Even though I have been painting for some time, I still find it difficult to get started – a plain white surface can be intimidating. However, you can gain confidence easily by simply applying the colours, then wiping out the design – the results are really quite dramatic! I particularly like painting flowers using this wiping out technique.

PAINTING FLOWERS ~ *White iris*

It is important to think about your composition and your colours before starting. Plan your design on paper first, and then prepare your palette. When wiping away the colours, it is not necessary to remove all the paint – leave some colour on the white surface to add shading and depth.

YOU WILL NEED

Bone china plate

Powder paints: light blue, pink, grey, light green, green, yellow ochre and iron red

Open medium

Wipe-out tool

Large square shader

Medium square shader

Small pointer brush

Blender brush

Tissues

Turpentine

Lint-free cloth

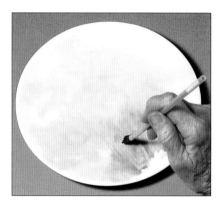

1. Paint the background area in blocks of colour with light blue, pink and a little grey using a large square shader. Work over the entire surface, filling in all the white areas. Waft over the surface using a blender brush to soften the effect.

2. Use a small pointer brush dipped in turpentine, or a wipe-out tool, to wipe out the outline of the design. Use a medium square shader dipped in turpentine and dried on a lint-free cloth to wipe away the colour from the petals. Work from the outside of the petals towards the centre of the flowers. Wipe the brush on the cloth between colours. Wipe out the stems and leaves using a small pointer brush. Fire at 780ºC (1435ºF).

3. Use greens to paint in the leaves, and iron red and yellow ochre for the flower centres. Add touches of yellow ochre and light blue and grey to the petals. Fire the plate again at 770ºC (1420ºF).

White iris   *The finished bone china plate*

Orchid on a porcelain plate
This plate already had silver lines on when purchased, so I painted the background all over with a medium square shader and blue-green paint, then sponged it with a fine cosmetic sponge. The silver lines were wiped clean with a wipe-out tool, and square shaders and a medium round brush were used to wipe out the flowers and leaves, leaving the trumpet centres and veins on the petals and leaves. The plate was fired at 820ºC (1510ºF).

Hibiscus on a bone china trinket box
A medium square shader was used to paint dark green over the box, and it was then sponged. The flower design was wiped out using a medium round brush, and the box was fired at 780ºC (1435ºF).

Poppies on a bone china plate

A large square shader was used to paint patches of iron red over the poppy areas; sections in between were filled in with strokes of yellow ochre, mauve, dark blue, light green, dark green and touches of brown. A medium square shader was used to wipe out the poppy petals, working from the outside edges inwards. Some paint was left as a base on which to build up the flower colours. The poppy centres were wiped clean and the black stamens painted in, then the seed heads, flower heads and their stems were wiped out. Light greens, yellow ochre and greys were then added and the plate was fired at 780ºC (1435ºF). More iron red and yellow ochre were added to deepen the colours on the flowers, and light green and black stamens were added to the centres. The background was enhanced, darker shades were added behind the poppies, and the stems were painted green. The plate was fired at 780ºC (1435ºF).

Hydrangeas on an earthenware tile
The areas behind the flower heads were painted with a large square shader, and complementary colours. Working from the bottom of the tile to the top, circular areas of blue with touches of mauve were applied, then blues and yellow, and finally pink was shaded with mauve. Green leaves were painted in, then a clean small square shader was used to wipe out the hydrangea petals. You could also use a wipe-out tool, but this occasionally produces a harsh effect. The pointed end of the wipe-out tool is ideal for taking away the stamens, which can then be coloured. Each floret has only four petals, but because there are so many of them I have only shown about six completed heads. The others can be painted in the background. Make sure they overlap each other and that leaves are tucked behind the petals. The tile was fired at 800ºC (1475ºF).

Roses on an earthenware tile

A large square shader was used to paint blocks of pale pink, deep pink, purple, blue and yellow with areas of light and dark green and brown over the background. The brush was cleaned and used to carefully wipe out the roses, leaving just a touch of colour. For each flower, the brush was drawn from the outer edge of the petals towards the flower centre, and pulled from left to right to form the base of the petals. Deeper colours were added towards the flower centres, and the outside curved edges of the petals were left lighter in shade. Light green and dark green were added to the leaves to create curved shapes. A blender brush was used to waft over the paintwork to soften the effect. The tile was fired at 800ºC (1475ºF). Deeper colours were added to the flowers and leaves and the tile was re-fired at 800ºC (1475ºF).

Pink clematis on an earthenware tile

A large square shader was used to paint patches of pink and mauve over the background areas where the flowers would be positioned. Light green, dark green and a few touches of brown were then added to the background, with some areas left free of colour. A clean, small square shader was used to wipe some of the colour out of the clematis flowers, the centres were wiped clean and the yellow stamens painted in. Some colour was wiped away from the leaves, and tendrils and stalks were added with the wipe-out tool. The tile was fired at 800ºC (1475ºF). More colour was added to the flowers, leaves, tendrils and stalks, and tones were deepened beneath the clematis heads and leaves. The tile was fired at 800ºC (1475ºF).

White clematis montana on a bone china plate.

Green and brown leaves were freely painted over a blue background using a large square shader. The flowers, buds, tendrils and stems were wiped out using a wipe-out tool and yellow was added to the flower centres. The brown stalks were painted and the plate fired at 780°C (1435°F). More colour was added in the flower centres, buds, tendrils, stalks and in background areas to define some of the leaves. The plate was fired at 780°C (1435°F).

OPPOSITE

Marigolds on an earthenware tile
This tile is based on the watercolour painting it is pictured with. A large square shader was used to paint free blocks of yellow ochre over the background behind the marigolds. The background area behind the stems was darkened using a clean brush and a mixture of dark blue, purple and dark brown. The colours were allowed to fade out towards the edges and touches of yellow ochre were added randomly to highlight the shade. A small square shader was dipped in turpentine, dried and then used to wipe out the flower heads, with strokes worked inwards from the outside edges. After wiping the centres clean, a medium round brush was used to wipe out the leaves, and a small pointer brush was used to wipe out the thin stalks. The tile was fired at 800°C (1475°F). The tile is pictured opposite at this stage.

The petals were then painted using iron red mixed with a little yellow ochre, and the colours were shaded from dark to light. The leaves were painted with grey, light green and yellow-green and darkened beneath the flower heads. The seed heads were added in light green and grey using a pointer brush. The tile was fired at 800°C (1475°F).

Daisies on an earthenware tile
A large square shader was used to paint light blue, dark blue, light green and dark green with some touches of yellow ochre over the surface, leaving a white edge. A medium round brush was used to wipe out the daisy petals around the yellow ochre centres, leaving just a touch of colour on the china surface. The daisies were wiped out quickly to capture the natural form of the flower. A pointer brush was loaded with light and dark green and run swiftly over the surface to indicate the stems and leaves. The tile was fired at 800°C (1475°F).

Using a pen

I have painted a number of pen, ink and wash watercolours over the years, and I have applied the same techniques to china surfaces with a great deal of success. Beautiful, delicate work can be painted using this technique, and mistakes just wiped out without any difficulty.

I use a mapping pen and pen oil which can be purchased from china painting suppliers. Pen oil is a clear liquid in a bottle. It is mixed with the powder paints using a palette knife to create an 'ink'. This ink air-dries fairly quickly so that, after a day, gentle washes of colour can be painted over your line work and the painting can be completed in one firing. However, it is better to fire the initial pen drawing first, to make sure that the colours will not run. Before using the whole palette, practise this technique with just one colour.

Clean pen nibs thoroughly after use. If they are just dipped into turpentine or water, they will clog up and the nib will rust in the holder. Take the pen apart and clean the nib, sleeve and holder thoroughly with methylated spirit, turpentine or the cleaner recommended by the manufacturer. Dry everything well.

1. Pen oil
For use with a pen. This is mixed, drop by drop, with powder paint and ground to the consistency of ink.

2. Icing sugar
This is mixed with hot water to make sugar water. It is used as an alternative to pen oil.

3. Powder paints
These are mixed with pen oil or sugar water.

4. Mapping pen
One with a strong steel nib for outlining.

5. Brushes
A selection of small brushes are used to complement penwork.

6. Tile
For mixing paints on.

MIXING THE PEN OIL

1. Place a small quantity of powder paint and a small quantity of pen oil separately on to a tile. Start mixing the two into an oily consistency. Grind well, adding more pen oil until the mixture resembles an inky puddle.

2. Turn the mapping pen upside down on the tile and carefully scoop the ink mixture up into the reservoir.

3. Hold the pen upright and practise letting the nib glide over the tile surface to make fine lines. Do not press down or the nib will be ruined. Pressing down can also make lines look thick and heavy.

It is best to work with fine lines and soft colours (above left). If penwork is too dark and heavy, the finished effect can look crude and overworked (above right). The inked lines will dominate the picture, and they can also affect the perspective, making the middle distance indistinct from the far distance.

USING A PEN AND A BRUSH ~ *Birds*

Do not try to cover the whole surface with penwork – it is best to just outline shapes with a pen and then use a brush to fill them in with soft colour. Try to avoid penwork in a sky, unless you want to indicate a distant bird. Clouds should not be outlined with pen, but should be defined with a brush.

YOU WILL NEED
Graphite carbon paper
Ballpoint pen or sharp pencil
Pen oil
Powder paint: deep blue
Mapping pen
Small pointer brush
Small square shader

1. Trace the design on to your china surface using graphite carbon paper and a ballpoint pen or sharp pencil (see page 16).

2. Mix two drops of pen oil with a little deep blue powder paint. Use a mapping pen to draw around the outline. While the sketch is still wet, paint in darker areas using a small pointer brush.

3. Use a small square shader to draw out the colour, and to fill in shaded areas.

Wrens and honeysuckle on a porcelain plate, by June Williams
June is a draftswoman and a meticulous artist. For this monochrome study, she worked out her design on paper first, then inked in the outlines. While the ink was still wet, she used a brush to blend in the colours. She then worked in darker colours using the ink straight from the palette. The plate was fired at 820ºC (1510ºF).

Mountain landscape on an earthenware tile

The mountains were outlined with fine penwork then left to dry for approximately one hour. The grasses on the distant shore were painted in, and those in the foreground were worked using ink. The trees and foliage were worked in more detail using both the pen and the brush. The tile was fired at 800ºC (1475ºF).

Sampler tile

This tile shows examples of realistic, traditional, Chinese and Japanese ways of working with a pen and shading areas with a brush.

Bone china butter dish

An outline sketch was drawn on the dish using a chinagraph pencil. It was then finely inked in with deep blue ink, and left to dry for approximately one hour. The ink mixture was ground again with a drop more oil and a small square shader was used to fill in the larger areas of the bird, flower and leaves. A small pointer brush was used for details such as the eye and legs. The dish was fired at 780ºC (1435ºF).

ADDING COLOUR ~ *Village scene*

Having learnt how to prepare a piece of china (see page 13), and practised the techniques on the previous pages, you are now ready to use more colours. Choose your design then transfer the outline of the picture on to the china using a chinagraph pencil. This project uses several colours, but black is avoided as it can look harsh and heavy.

1. Draw the outline of your design using a fine mapping pen and yellow ochre, green, light brown and dark brown ink (see pages 36–38). Fire at 780ºC (1435ºF).

2. Lay in the sky using a large square shader and a mixture of light and dark blue. Leave white areas for the clouds. Wipe out selected cloud areas with a medium square shader (see page 26), softening the edges as you work. Wipe paint away from the edge of the plate to create a white border.

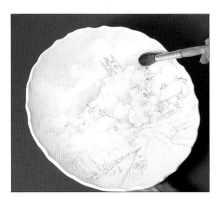

3. Add a touch of grey and mauve to the blues and lay in the distant hills with a medium square shader. Use a blender brush to gently waft over the horizon and hills. This will blend in the colours and soften the brush strokes.

4. Use a small square shader and greens, yellows and browns to build up the trees. Work from light to dark and gently blend and shade colours into each other. Add shades of grey to the roofs of the houses, and use browns and greens to paint in the ducks. Fire the plate at 780ºC (1435ºF).

Village scene *The finished bone china plate*

Town Hall, Market Place, Wokingham on an earthenware tile, designed and painted by Mac Collingwood
Brickwork and tiling can be indicated with just a few lines. Here, only the main outlines were inked in, and then washes of colour were painted on. The tile was fired at 800ºC (1475ºF).

Wren and bracken on a porcelain plate
This plate had the gold lines on it when I bought it. The design was penned in using light brown. Pale colours were painted first, then the plate was fired at 820ºC (1510ºF). Deeper colours and details were added and the plate was fired at 810ºC (1490ºF).

Poppy and swan on a bone china plate

The main outline of the design was sketched, then a fine pen was used with dark green ink to lightly draw in textures on the tree trunks and foliage. The flowers were drawn in and more detail was brought in on the foreground tree. The swans' beaks were drawn using fine lines, their necks and bodies were outlined, and ripples were drawn on the surface of the lake to suggest movement. The plate was then fired at 780ºC (1435ºF). The sky was washed with blue paint and the clouds were wiped out. Yellow was blended into the distant sky to add light to the painting. The tree foliage was coloured lightly, and the bridge and stone bank were painted in. The water was painted from dark to light. Colours were added to the swans, and white reflections were created in the water by wiping away the colour. Finally, the foreground flowers and leaves were painted in. The plate was fired at 780ºC (1435ºF).

Mr Snail's Regatta on a bone china plate

The design was first drawn on to the plate using a chinagraph pencil, and then toning outlines were penned in using colours to complement the main shades. Ripples were painted around the boats. The plate was fired at 780ºC (1435ºF). A medium square shader was used to paint the sky and water. A small round brush was used to paint the regatta scene, the big poppy and the foreground flowers. The plate was fired at 780ºC (1435ºF).

Reproduced by kind permission of The Porcelain Artist's Magazine

SWIRLS ~ *Leaping fish*

This technique started by accident! I had often watched my students wiping off paintings they were not pleased with. I then realised that the colours could be worked into each other instead of wiping them out completely, to produce interesting patterns. This technique allows you to really let your imagination roam, and scenes often develop as you work.

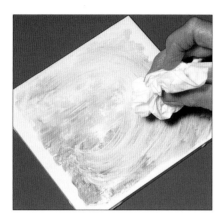

YOU WILL NEED

Earthenware tile

Powder paints: dark green, turquoise, mauve, yellow and light blue

Open medium

Large square shader

Tissue

Tracing paper or acetate

Mapping pen

Pen oil

1. Lay in background colours of dark green, turquoise, mauve, yellow and light blue using a large square shader. Use a crumpled tissue to swirl the colours around, softly dab them and gently wipe out areas. Experiment with the pattern until you are pleased with the result. Fire at 800ºC (1475ºF).

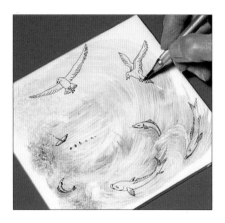

2. Look at the background design from all angles until you see an image begin to materialise. Make sketches on tracing paper or acetate using the mapping pen, then place these on top of the background. Use the mapping pen and pen oil mixed with dark green powder paint to draw in your design. Fire at 780ºC (1435ºF).

The finished earthenware tile

44

Convolvulus on an earthenware tile
Dark blue, pink and mauve were painted on to a tile and wiped round with a tissue to create an impression of a view into a tunnel. I used a small square shader to wipe out the areas of paint where the convolvulus flowers would fall. The tile was then fired at 800ºC (1475ºF). A small cottage was drawn into the far end of the tunnel using pen and ink. The swirls of paint were used as guidelines to create a tangle of flowers and leaves, and to give the impression of looking through the tunnel to the image beyond. A little more green was added to the leaves, and a very light green wash to the flowers. The tile was then fired at 780ºC (1435ºF).

Kingfisher and frog on an earthenware tile
Light blue, green, yellow and light brown were painted on to the background using a large square shader. A tissue was used to wipe the paint round to create a wave of colour, and the result was a steep hill, with a pool in the valley. The tile was fired at 800ºC (1475ºF). Contour lines were drawn into the hill and around the pool and the rocks were outlined using brown and green ink. The trees in the far distance were lightly penned in. The kingfisher and frog were drawn in with ink, then painted. A light wash was applied over the trees and the sun was painted. The tile was fired at 780ºC (1435ºF).

RUNNING GROUND ~ *Underwater scene*

As with the swirling backgrounds, this is pure fantasy work. Turpentine is run through wet paint and the resulting colours and patterns can be used as a background for all sorts of images – animals, fish, landscapes, waterscapes and much more. I spent a great deal of time underwater diving while living in Singapore, and this inspired me to use blues and greens when practising the running ground technique. The resulting patterns looked just like underwater scenes. Developing the images in this type of painting is so exciting – as the picture evolves, you will find your imagination is captured by the underwater shapes. For this project you should choose a limited palette of colours – blues, greens and yellows; blues, pinks and greys; or browns, yellows and greens.

> **YOU WILL NEED**
> Earthenware tile
> Pipette
> Small scroller brush
> Large square shader
> Turpentine
> Mapping pen
> Pen oil
> Powder paints: dark green, light green, blue and yellow
> Open medium

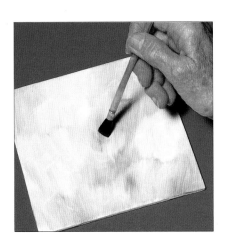

1. Use a large square shader to paint stripes and blocks of colour all over a white tile.

2. Dribble clean turpentine across the tile at an angle using a pipette or a small scroller brush.

3. If you see an image begin to appear, emphasise it with a subtle wipe of a small scroller brush.

4. Build up your design until you are happy with the results. Fire at 800ºC (1475ºF).

5. Use fine dark green penwork to draw around the shapes and emphasise the images. Fire at 800ºC (1475ºF)

Coral and seaweed on an earthenware tile
This tile uses the same colours as the one shown in the demonstration opposite. Background colours were laid down and then turpentine was dribbled over. The tile was fired at 800ºC (1475ºF). The fish, coral and seaweed were worked up on the fired base using a pen and dark green ink. Colours were added and deepened to add depth to the picture. The tile was fired at 800ºC (1475ºF).

Fairy forest painting on an earthenware tile, owned by Sophie Williams
Turpentine was run across the surface of the painted tile, and tiny drops were put in the foreground. The tile was fired at 800ºC (1475ºF). Penwork was applied to create the trees and penwork texture was added for the leaves and tree trunks. Mushrooms were created by penning around the circles formed by the drops of turpentine. The tile was fired at 800ºC (1475ºF).

Working with lustres

Islamic artisans used lustres over a white tin glaze early in the tenth century. The technique spread to Europe much later and it was not until the early nineteenth century that lustre decoration became popular in Britain. Platinum was often used instead of silver because it did not tarnish, and this was later developed into a pink and purple lustre. During the Victorian period in Britain, the technique gained in popularity. Jugs and mugs covered in deep copper lustres were fashionable and could be easily acquired. Lustre was popular too on bone china, but few pieces can now be traced as they were poorly marked at the time.

Lustres are metallic salts which are used to colour china. They can be bought ready-mixed in bottles from specialist suppliers. The salts are combined with resin, bismuth and oils. When fired, the resin and oils burn away, and a thin film of coloured metal is left on the glazed surface.

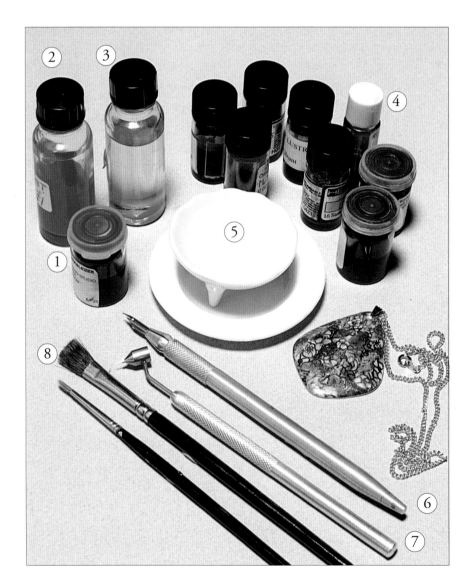

1. Marbling liquid
This is used over lustres when touch dry to create random marbled patterns.

2. Peelable resist
This is used to mask off areas from lustre.

3. Lustre thinner
This can be used to clean brushes and sponges used with lustre, or to create patterns on surfaces painted with lustre.

4. Lustres
Very shiny translucent colours that fire into the glaze of china.

5. Tiny dish or saucer
Used to mix or thin lustres in.

6. Mapping pen
A mapping pen with a strong nib should be used for outlining.

7. Reservoir pen
This is filled with liquid bright gold to give a thin uniform line.

8. Brushes
A selection of small brushes are used to apply the lustre.

USING LUSTRE COLOURS

Lustres come in shades of brown and amber, and it is only after they are fired that they take on their colour, and the beautiful iridescent shades become apparent. It is therefore a good idea to test out your colours before you start. Keep your own record on a tile and experiment with colours. Remember that lustres can be overlaid to create different effects.

Lustres come in a whole spectrum of colours, but a good basic range is shown right. The following colours will harmonise to create lovely effects:

• Pink, red, lilac, dark blue

• Light blue, turquoise, dark blue

• Yellow, mid-green, dark green, blue-green

• Yellow, peach, golden brown and copper

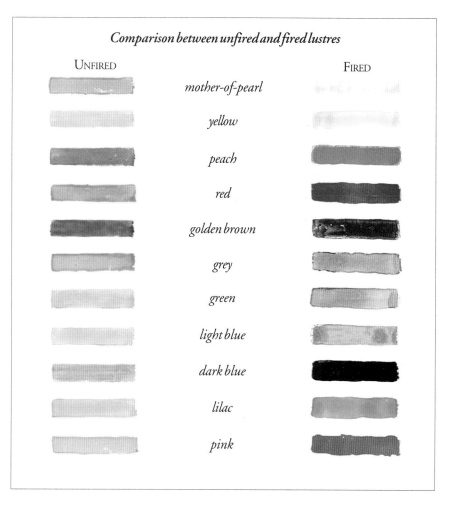

Comparison between unfired and fired lustres

UNFIRED		FIRED
	mother-of-pearl	
	yellow	
	peach	
	red	
	golden brown	
	grey	
	green	
	light blue	
	dark blue	
	lilac	
	pink	

NOTE

• Grey can be used to tone down strong colours.

• A thin black lustre becomes charcoal after firing. If laid over a strong, fired red it will become dark maroon.

• Turquoise blue over fired pink becomes violet blue.

• Pale blue over fired yellow-green becomes jade green.

• Orange over fired cinnamon or light brown becomes burnt orange.

• Apply mother-of-pearl lustre in wiggles using a shader brush – this will bring out the iridescence when it is fired.

• Mother-of-pearl can be painted over any fired lustre including gold, copper, platinum, bronze and black, to produce iridescent effects.

• Platinum fired and then covered with a light green, blue or yellow lustre, then fired again, produces a lovely iridescent effect.

• Two drops of lilac added to mother-of-pearl create a translucent colour; drops of green or blue added to mother-of-pearl create a watery effect.

FREE PAINTING

Many different effects can be created with lustres – they can be applied smoothly, sponged on, 'floated on', or applied from light to dark. They can also be marbled, haloed, dribbled, pressed with cling film or streaked with a stiff brush. Always clean the brushes carefully with lustre thinner or the suppliers' recommended cleaner between each application of colour. The first firing should be no higher than 760ºC (1400ºF) if bone china or 780ºC (1435ºF) if porcelain, and the second 740ºC (1365ºF) if bone china, or 750ºC (1380ºF) if porcelain.

Lovely free effects are easy to create. The bone china heart-shaped trinket box and the tall bone china vase opposite have had patches of lustres randomly painted on. They were then fired at 760ºC (1400ºF), and shapes were then outlined with gold to create flowers and leaves. For more information on the application of gold, see pages 56–59.

DIPPING IN WATER

Beautiful effects can be achieved quickly and easily by 'floating' the lustre colours on water. To do this, fill an old plastic container with cold water and then use a fine paintbrush to carefully place a few drops of lustre on the surface of the water. Add a second lustre, then a third. Remember to use compatible colours (see page 49). The lustre will float on the water and can be swirled round gently. Dip the china on to the water, touching the surface so that the colours are picked up. Remove it and leave to dry thoroughly. You can then clean off the back or any part that should not have lustre on it using the tip of a cocktail stick covered with cotton wool and dipped in lustre thinner or methylated spirit. Fire at 760ºC (1400ºF).

DRIBBLING

Paint or dab compatible lustre colours on to the china. Before they dry, dribble or dot methylated spirit or lustre thinner over the surface. A little lavender oil has a lovely softening effect if dribbled over painted areas, and oils can be moved about the surface if you blow on them with a straw – this will create interesting effects.

Once the design has been fired, it can be enhanced with lines, circles and dots of gold or platinum. Fire at 760ºC (1400ºF).

USING MARBLING LIQUID

Carefully paint lustre colours on to the china. When they are dry, gently brush marbling liquid over the whole coloured area. Do not overwork brush strokes that have been laid on, or the paintbrush will lift off the lustre. Interesting cobweb effects can be created with copper, gold and platinum using this technique. Fire at 760ºC (1400ºF). The heat of the kiln creates the broken pattern in this technique.

Bone china trinket box
Blue, green, light brown and orange lustres were painted on to the box, then lustre thinner was dropped on. It was fired at 760ºC (1400ºF). The scene that emerged was built up using dark green penwork. It was fired at 750ºC (1380ºF).

A selection of objects that have been decorated with lustre using free painting techniques.

Trinket boxes

The lids and the bases of the two boxes were skimmed over the top of water containing different coloured lustres. They were fired at 760ºC (1400ºF). One of the boxes was covered with gold penwork to pick out all the different lustre colours and shapes. It was then fired again at 740ºC (1365ºF).

Blue porcelain vase

This has light blue and dark blue, mauve and mother-of-pearl lustres painted on in patches. Lustre thinner was dropped on with a brush to give a 'dribbled' effect. The base of the vase and the inside were then wiped clean. The vase was fired at 760ºC (1400ºF). The shapes were outlined with platinum penwork and fired at 760ºC (1400ºF).

Brown porcelain vase

This has been painted with peach, golden brown and copper lustre and allowed to dry. Marbling liquid was carefully painted over the colours, leaving the lustres beneath intact. The vase was then fired at 760ºC (1400ºF).

Porcelain brooch

Patches of pink, blue, and green lustre were brushed on. Lustre thinner was dropped on and the brooch was then fired at 760ºC (1400ºF). The shapes that formed were turned into flowers and leaves by outlining in platinum using a pen, and by drawing in stamens, flower centres and leaf veins. The brooch was fired at 750ºC (1380ºF).

Bone china pomander

Light blue, dark blue, pink, lilac and green lustres were painted on in patches. Lustre thinner was dropped on and it was then fired at 760ºC (1400ºF). All the shapes were outlined with platinum penwork to create flowers and leaves. The pomander was fired at 750ºC (1380ºF).

CONTROLLED PAINTING~ *Leaves*

The wonderful luminosity and iridescence of lustres make them ideal for many different types of design including fantasy scenes, seascapes, leaves, flowers, berries, insects and butterflies. Even simple patterns and designs take on a shimmering beauty. For example, a picture of a fairy would be enhanced if her wings were painted with a mother-of-pearl lustre. If you make a mistake with the colour of your lustre, you can sometimes rectify it by applying a darker lustre on top.

When sketching on to the china surface, do not use chinagraph, graphite or carbon pencils as they can leave a residue beneath the lustre. Use a fine felt-tip pen.

YOU WILL NEED

Porcelain vase

Fine felt-tip pen

Lustres: green, peach, light brown, brown and dark pink

Liquid bright gold

Lustre thinner

Fine cosmetic sponges

Reservoir pen

Small square shader

Tissue

NOTE

You can outline a design in gold first, and then fire it. A light lustre can then be painted over the top of the fired lines to create an iridescent metallic gold effect.

If you make a mistake when outlining in gold, try rubbing vigorously with a gold eraser to remove or tone down unwanted areas of gold.

Use a fine felt-tip pen to mark out a lustre design. A chinagraph pencil can leave a faint white line once fired.

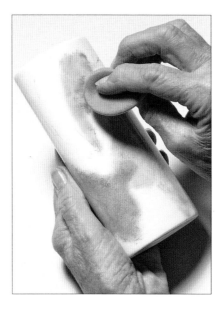

1. Lightly sketch a leaf design on to the china surface using a fine felt-tip pen. Use a small square shader to apply green, peach, brown and dark pink lustres to the leaves. Vary the colours, shading in deeper colours down the middle of each leaf towards the tip. Sponge over any painted areas, using a different sponge over each colour.

2. Use a clean sponge to lay in a light brown background. Let the lustre dry completely before cleaning off unwanted lustre with a tissue and lustre thinner or methylated spirit. Fire the vase at 760°C (1400°F). Add more lustres to strengthen or change the colours, then fire again at 750°C (1380°F). Finally, outline the leaves and draw in the veins using a reservoir pen and liquid bright gold straight from the pot. Fire at 740°C (1365°F).

Leaves on a bone china trinket box
The design was drawn on to the surface and the white areas were masked out using peelable resist. Copper lustre was painted carefully over the background around the leaves and allowed to dry. The peelable resist was removed and the box was fired at 760ºC (1400ºF). The leaves were painted using brown, green, yellow, carmine and peach lustres. The box was fired at 760ºC (1400ºF). A second coat of copper lustre was applied and the box was fired at 760ºC (1400ºF). All the leaves were outlined with liquid bright gold using a reservoir pen. The box was fired at 750ºC (1380ºF).

Leaves on a porcelain vase
The leaves were sketched on using a fine felt-tip pen and lustre colours were sponged and painted on using browns, orange, red and green. A light brown background was sponged on and the vase was fired at 780°C (1435°F). The leaves were outlined with gold, and veins and texture were added to the centres. The vase was fired at 770°C (1420°F).

Butterflies on bone china trinket box
The butterflies on this box were coloured with lustres for the first firing at 760°C (1400°F). Fine lines were added using a small pointer brush and the box was fired at 760°C (1400°F). Finally, the whole box was covered with a coat of mother-of-pearl using a small square shader. The box was fired at 750°C (1380°F).

Porcelain butterflies
Different coloured lustres were painted on to the wings and bodies and the butterflies were then fired at 780°C (1435°F). Details were then picked out with gold , copper or platinum lustres, and the butterflies were fired at 760°C (1400°F).

Painting with gold

Using gold is a little more expensive than using other china paints, but the results are beautiful – they are mellow and rich, without being garish and you can choose a shiny or a matt finish. There are no limits to the type of design you can use – choose anything from strong gold backgrounds to subtle, finely finished gold details in a delicate picture. Birds, flowers, landscapes and abstract designs all lend themselves to being decorated with gold.

Gold requires an undercoat before it is applied to the surface of the china. An even coat of yellow ochre or pink beneath bright gold gives a shiny finish. Gold base is a good ground as it gives a matt finish which has the appearance of burnished gold, even when liquid bright gold is painted over it. Alternatively, you could apply two coats of gold. Brush on the first coat, smooth out the surface using a sponge, then fire at 760°C (1400°F). Apply a second coat and fire again at the same temperature.

Burnishing gold is dull when fired. It should be polished with a fibreglass brush, a special burnishing pad or fine damp sand (supplied by china painting suppliers) to bring up the shine.

1. Gold, platinum and copper liquid paints

A selection of metallic paints are available. Liquid bright gold is pre-mixed and can be painted over a base coat. Liquid burnishing gold can also be used, but it requires polishing after firing. Copper and platinum can be used to outline details.

2. Peelable resist

This is used to mask areas

3. Yellow ochre and pink paint

These can be used as a base coat underneath gold paint.

4. Gold base

This can be used as a base coat underneath gold paint.

5. Brushes

A selection of small synthetic brushes can be used to apply gold.

Clematis on bone china vase

The design was drawn on with a chinagraph pencil. Mauve was applied to the top of the vase with a large square shader. A sponge was used to soften the colour. The leaves and flowers at the top of the vase were painted with a base coat of pink. The flowers on the lower part were given a coat of light pink, yellow centres were added, then green leaves and stems were painted in. The vase was fired at 780ºC (1435ºF).

A second coat of mauve was sponged on. Deeper shades of pink were added to the flowers on the lower part of the vase, together with a little light brown in the flower centres, and a darker brown for the stamens. Dark green was added to the leaves. The vase was fired at 780ºC (1435ºF).

Peelable resist was painted around the flowers and the leaves at the top of the vase, then these areas were filled in with liquid bright gold. A clean sponge was used to soften the gold. When the paint was dry, the resist was lifted off with a cocktail stick. The vase was fired at 760ºC (1400ºF).

The petals were outlined and the veins and stamens were drawn in using a fine nib and deep pink ink. Dark green ink was used for the leaves. Green was painted into the centre of the leaves and pink into the petals. The vase was fired at 760ºC (1400ºF).

PAINTING ON TOP OF GOLD ~ *Convolvulus*

This is a technique that allows you to paint colours directly on to a surface you have already painted gold. Colour can be built up and lines can be added, allowing a subtle glint of gold to come through. This will enrich a design. When preparing your gold surface, remember that you can use gold base under gold instead of the undercoat of yellow ochre or pink.

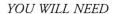

Convolvulus *The finished porcelain trinket box*

1. Trace your design on to the lid of the box (see page 16) or draw it freehand using a chinagraph pencil.

YOU WILL NEED

Porcelain trinket box

Tracing paper, sharp pencil or ballpoint pen

Graphite carbon paper

Small square shader (synthetic)

Small pointer brush

Powder paints: Pink, yellow ochre, light green, dark green and brown

Open medium

Liquid bright gold

Mapping pen

Pen oil

Fine cosmetic sponge

Peelable resist

Cocktail stick

2. Use a small square shader to apply an undercoat of yellow ochre or pink to the flowers, buds and leaves you want to cover with gold. Paint the background yellow ochre, then shade it out to light green. Paint in a brown border, then sponge it to soften the effect. Fire at 820ºC (1510ºF).

3. Use a small synthetic square shader to paint peelable resist around the design. Allow to dry. Use liquid bright gold and a small synthetic square shader to paint in the flowers, leaves and stems. Sponge the surface to create an even finish. Leave to dry, then use a cocktail stick to peel off the resist. Fire at 760ºC (1400ºF).

4. Use a pen and dark green ink to outline the flowers and leaves and to add central veins. Leave to dry, then use a small pointer brush to work in green paint over the penwork to add depth. Fire at 760ºC (1400ºF).

Hibiscus on a bone china plate
The design was drawn on with a chinagraph pencil and peelable resist was applied to the flowers and leaves that would be gold. Iron red was used for the central flower and bud, and light blue and yellow were painted softly on to the background. The light green leaves were painted, and a grey-green was used to shade the outside edges. The resist was peeled off and the plate was then fired at 780ºC (1435ºF). Resist was painted around the flowers and leaves that were to be gold. The first coat of gold was painted in, the surface was sponged over and then it was allowed to dry. The peelable resist was peeled off then the plate was fired at 760ºC (1400ºF). A second coat of gold was applied and the plate was fired again at 760ºC (1400ºF). A pen and red ink were used for the lines on the gold petals, and green ink was used on the leaves. When dry, dark brown was shaded into the flower contours. The plate was fired at 760ºC (1400ºF).

Working with relief

Beautiful textured effects can be created if you use white relief pastes. Different types of paste are available depending on what surface you are working on. I suggest that you use special thinners and mediums with these products and always read the manufacturers' instructions.

The pastes are available as white powders which, when mixed with the oil supplied by the manufacturer, can be applied to a porcelain, bone china or earthenware surface. They can also be mixed with fat oil and pure turpentine. Pre-mixed pastes are also available.

1. Relief enamel powder

This is mixed with relief oil to form a paste. It is used on bone china or earthenware.

2. Raised paste powder

This is mixed with relief oil to form a paste. It is used on porcelain, bone china and earthenware.

3. Pre-mixed raised paste

This is available from specialist suppliers. It is used on porcelain, bone china and earthenware.

4. Relief oil

This is mixed with relief enamel powder, raised paste powder or I-relief to form a paste.

5. Powder paint

This can be used to colour relief paste.

6. Tile

Relief enamel powder, raised paste powder or I-relief should be mixed with relief oil on a tile.

7. Palette knife

Use a palette knife to mix the relief enamel powder, raised paste powder or I-relief with relief oil.

8. Brushes

A selection of small brushes can be used to apply relief.

RAISED PASTE AND I-RELIEF

These are white powders, both suitable for relief work on porcelain, bone china and earthenware. Each can be mixed with relief oil. I-relief can also be mixed with skimmed milk to create a thicker mixture that you can use to build up height. Both can be coloured with a few grains of powder paint if required. Uncoloured raised paste fires to a shiny white, and the I-relief fires to an ivory semi-matt finish.

When mixed carefully with a palette knife, the paste can be picked up with the blade, or a fine brush. When it is dropped gently on to china, it will form a string. A cocktail stick or a fine brush can be used to drop dome-like dots on to the china. The relief paste has to dry thoroughly before it is fired. When using these pastes, porcelain must be fired at 820°C (1510°F), bone china at 780°C (1435°F) and earthenware at 800°C (1475°F).

RELIEF ENAMEL

This is a white powder that can only be used on bone china or earthenware. It will not adhere safely to porcelain, and dots will pop off during firing. It is mixed with relief oil and should form a string when applied to the china surface. Relief enamel is also available ready-mixed in kit and tube form from specialist china suppliers, so that dots or lines can be applied straight on to the china, as if you were icing a cake. This method is quicker and easier than using a brush. It can be coloured with powder paint. Uncoloured relief enamel fires to a glossy pure white finish. It has to dry thoroughly before firing. Bone china should be fired at 780°C (1435°F) and earthenware at 800°C (1475°F).

> *NOTE*
>
> Relief enamel powder, raised paste powder and I-relief are all mixed with relief oil to make a paste. The paste should be the consistency of toothpaste. Use a tile to mix on and a palette knife to mix with.
>
> The mixed paste should flatten out slightly when dropped on to the surface of the tile. If it spreads too much, add a little more powder. If it forms peaks, add a little more oil.

TECHNIQUES WITH RELIEF

There are lots of ways of using relief. It can be applied with a brush, a cocktail stick, or it can be piped on. Experiment to create different effects.

Clockwise from top right:
Applying raised lines with a cocktail stick.

Applying dots with a small scroller brush.

Applying scrolls with one stroke of a small scroller brush.

Dragging over the edge of a line of paste using a small square shader. This will soften the edge of the line.

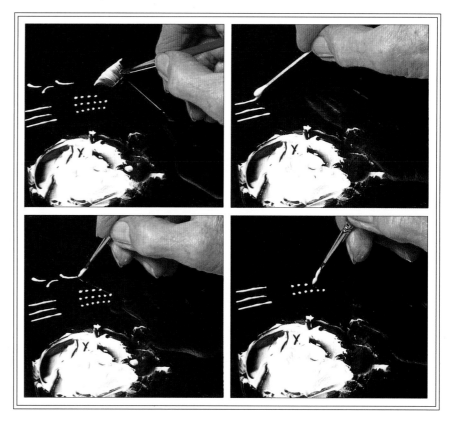

Tiger lily on a brown glazed earthenware tile
Dots of relief paste can be used in many different ways. Any subject can be 'drawn' in this way – animals, birds, trees and so on. Flowers look particularly effective on dark backgrounds. Here, a small pointer brush has been used to drop the outline of dots on to the tile. Lots of dots were placed on the highlighted areas on the petals, to give an impression of light. Very few dots were placed on the shaded areas. It was fired at 800ºC (1475ºF).

Butterflies on an earthenware tile
A swirled background was created (see page 44) and the tile was fired at 800ºC (1475ºF). Butterflies were drawn on to tracing paper, then cut out and arranged over the painted background. I wanted to give the impression of butterflies flying into a tunnel of grass and flowers. Once the design was finalised, the butterflies were transferred on to the surface using carbon paper. Relief enamel paste was carefully applied over the traced forms using a small square shader. A little of the background was allowed to show through the wings; more relief paste was used to thicken the bodies and heads and the edges of the wings, and dots were used to add detail. The tile was fired at 800ºC (1475ºF).

Raised paste on a porcelain plate
A shaded background was created by brushing blues and greens on to the surface, then fading them out to white. The plate was fired at 820ºC (1510ºF). Dots, scrolls and lines of white and coloured raised paste were dropped on in a wave-like design. The plate was fired at 800ºC (1475ºF).

ABSTRACT DESIGNS~ *Aerial view*

White or coloured relief enamel can be used over any painted design to enhance shapes and forms, or to embellish abstract designs. Here, I show how to apply a free-form dot pattern over different colours and shapes. The dots create a jewelled effect reminiscent of the stylised jewelled porcelain of the Victorian era. The inspiration for the background came from a lovely book I was given, which was full of extraordinary aerial views from around the world.

Relief enamel can be used to complement abstract designs. This demonstration uses uncoloured paste, but you can colour it using powder paint to complement the colour of your background design.

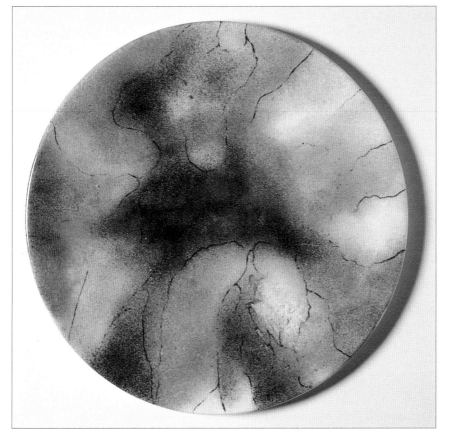

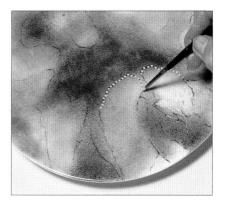

1. Apply patches of yellow, green, orange, mid-brown, iron red and dark brown with a medium square shader. When the painting is finished, sponge the plate all over with a cosmetic sponge. Fire at 780ºC (1435ºF). Use a chinagraph pencil to draw lines between areas of colour.

2. Mix the relief enamel powder to a toothpaste consistency with the relief oil (see page 61). Use a small scroller brush to pick up some paste and apply it to the painted china surface. Continue until all the lines are covered. Fire at 780ºC (1435ºF).

OPPOSITE
Relief enamel paste can be used over abstract designs to create striking effects. These are just a few examples of how the designs can be emphasised with relief enamel paste.

PÂTE SUR PÂTE

This technique was perfected by French designer Louis Marc Salon at Sèvres in 1862. He went on to join the Minton factory in England in 1870. The method that he used required excellent skills, although it was as laborious as it was time-consuming. Slip (liquid clay) was built up in layers on coloured, damp, unfired ware, until it was thick enough for the artist to carve the work as a bas-relief. This was then given its first firing (bisque), which was followed by a final glaze firing. An alternative method was employed by Wedgewood, where contrasting colour decorations were casts taken from moulds, which were sprigged on to the surface of the ware while it was still damp. The results of these two methods are similar, but only Salon was able to create beautiful translucent effects with his thin slip applications.

The methods employed by china painters today are much simpler and quicker. Relief paste is painted on to a dark ground which is applied to finished glazed ware. You can buy pre-coloured china to work on or you can groundlay your own background on to plain white china (see pages 74–75) then fire it at 800ºC (1475ºF).

Mix up the relief paste as shown on page 61, but use a little more oil that you would normally, to obtain a thinner consistency. If this thinned mixture of the paste is used, the background will show through, giving the picture a translucency. If used more thickly, you can build up a relief effect.

The paste dries quickly, and more layers can easily be added to give greater depth. Make sure your work is absolutely dry before firing it.

Flowers on a grey earthenware tile
These leaves, leaf turn-overs and petals were created by painting the paste thickly and dragging up the edge so that it stood proud of the china.
Alternatively, a scroll of paste could have been laid in then dragged towards the centre of the leaf, or to where the petal joins the centre of the flower. In the case of the Chinese lantern, the paste was dragged sideways. The tile was fired at 800ºC (1475ºF).

Wave on a deep blue earthenware tile
The design was outlined with a chinagraph pencil. White relief enamel paste was painted thinly on to the design with a medium square shader. The enamel was thickened on the crests of the waves and pulled into points with a small pointer brush. Dots of enamel were added to create spray. The leaping fish and the bird were painted in. The enamel was left to dry, and then the tile was fired at 800ºC (1475ºF).

Birds on a grey earthenware tile
The feathers were painted in with relief paste and pulled up towards the leading wing edge. More paste was picked up with the brush and another line of feathers was laid in further up, and pulled up to the same edge. The whites of the eyes and the beak were dropped in so that they looked opaque. The tile was fired at 800ºC (1475ºF).

OPPOSITE

Fairies, birds and flowers on earthenware tiles
These designs were planned and then traced on to the surface of each pre-coloured tile. Relief powder was mixed with relief oil until it had the consistency of thick cream. The paste was ground and mixed well, using a palette knife. A small scroller brush was used to carefully paint the design. The paste was used thickly and thinly to create tones. The tiles were allowed to dry thoroughly. They were fired at 800ºC (1475ºF).

Birds and leaves on a bone china plate
The design was worked out carefully and then transferred on to a bought blue and white plate using a chinagraph pencil. Relief enamel paste was then applied and the plate was fired at 780ºC (1435ºF).

OPPOSITE

Birds and feathers on porcelain pots
I-relief was applied thinly in areas, then it was worked more thickly over the birds' bodies, the trees and the foliage to create texture. A thin mixture of paste was applied to create the clouds, and it was then softened with a sponge. The pots were fired at 820ºC (1510ºF). The cranes were painted with platinum and the pot was fired at 760ºC (1400ºF).

Modern Techniques

Now is the time to experiment, to do something different and to create your own designs! Modern materials and techniques can be combined with traditional methods to produce innovative, unique pieces. You can work on porcelain, bone china or earthenware for most of the techniques; however, flaking powder is not suitable for use on earthenware or bone china.

In general, large items are not suitable for these techniques as the finished decoration can look garish, whereas similar designs on small plates, tiles, boxes or jewellery blanks can look beautiful. Delicate linear or painted designs can be applied over textured or gold surfaces to create wonderful effects.

You can use all the techniques I have covered so far in this book to create your own designs. Glass and beads can be laid into some relief paste mixtures to embellish patterns and designs, or skimmed milk can be added and the paste worked up into interesting shapes.

1. Raised paste

Stones can be embedded into raised paste.

2. Relief oil

This is mixed with relief enamel or raised paste powder to form a paste.

3. Flaking powder

This powder is used to remove the glaze and add texture that way. It can only be used on porcelain. After firing, the rough surface is chipped off with a knife. The textured surface can then be gilded, or painted with platinum or lustre.

The powder is mixed with either water, milk or a medium. Glass or sand can be embedded in the mixture to embellish the texture.

4. Relief enamel

This is used to add relief on bone china or earthenware. It is mixed with relief oil to form a paste.

5. Peelable resist

This is available in liquid form and is applied with a synthetic brush. It is used to mask out areas that you want to remain white, or those that you wish to work on after the first firing.

6. Groundlay oil

Powder paints are applied over groundlay oil to produce a velvety texture.

7. Milk

This is mixed with flaking powder to make a paste, or with I-relief to make a thickly textured paste.

8. Structure powder

This is similar to I-relief, and can be used on porcelain.

9. I-Relief

This is used on porcelain to create relief.

10. Powder paints

You can add powder paint to relief enamel, I-relief or raised paste to colour the relief work.

11. Metallic powder paints

These are lovely soft velvet powders that are available in a range of colours, including gold and silver. They are best put on as a grounding, or they can be painted on. If you choose the latter technique, use two coats of colour, and fire after each application. Fire at 820ºC (1510ºF) if porcelain, 780ºC (1435ºF) if bone china, or 800ºC (1475ºF) if an earthenware tile.

12. Gold, platinum and copper liquid precious metals

These are pre-mixed. They can be used to outline. Liquid bright gold should be used over a base coat.

13. Silk and sponge

Fine silk is used over a sponge to prepare the groundlay

14. Tweezers

For picking up pieces of glass or beads.

15. Scraper tool

This can be used to scrape off small mistakes made in gold or platinum.

16. Broken glass, glass beads, glass pearls, glass lumps

These are available from china painting suppliers.

17. Knife

This is used to chip off flaking powder once it has been fired.

18. Palette knife

This is used to mix relief pastes.

19. Brushes

A selection of brushes are used for modern techniques.

GROUNDLAYING ~ *Floral swirl*

Groundlaying gives a completely opaque finish on a design, and I frequently use it when working with modern techniques. You can use either liquid metallic or powder paints. If powder paints are used as a grounding, they should be applied over groundlay oil. Here I show you how to mask out an area, how to lay down a ground, and finally how to use flaking powder.

YOU WILL NEED

Porcelain brooch

Chinagraph pencil

Peelable resist

Groundlay oil

Small piece of sponge

Natural silk

Elastic band

Blender brush

Small pointer brush

2 small square shaders (synthetic)

Powder paints: iron red, green, yellow ochre, dark brown and metallic red-gold

Open medium

Copper lustre

Mask

Flaking powder

Milk

Palette knife

Cocktail stick

Knife

Protective goggles

Methylated spirit

1. Draw your design on to the brooch with a chinagraph pencil. Mask the area that will remain white using a peelable resist and a small synthetic square shader. Leave to dry.

2. Cover your work surface with clean paper, then place the brooch on top. Use a small synthetic square shader to apply groundlay oil to the surface. Leave for fifteen minutes. Cover a small piece of sponge with natural silk and secure with an elastic band. Use this to pad the groundlay oil on the brooch. Continue padding until the oiliness disappears.

3. Use a blender brush to dust the red-gold metallic powder paint on to the area where you have applied groundlay oil.

NOTE

Wear a mask when groundlaying with powder paint, as the powder contained within it is very fine.

As an alternative to the groundlaying technique, you could use decals (transfers), which are now available from specialist suppliers. These come in a range of colours, and can be cut out to fit the piece of china you are working on.

4. Use the blender brush to push the powder over the surface so that the groundlay area is completely covered and the surface looks like velvet. Brush off any excess powder. This can be used again.

5. Mix some flaking powder with a little milk until it is the consistency of whipped cream. Use a thicker paste if you want to achieve a more textured effect.

6. Push the flaking powder on to the surface using a small synthetic square shader.

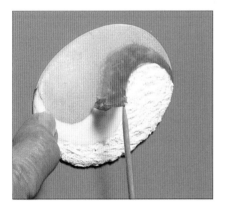

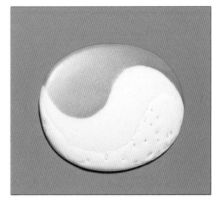

7. Carefully peel away the resist using a cocktail stick.

8. Fire the brooch at 820°C (1510°F).

9. Use a knife to chip away the flaking powder to reveal a textured surface. It is advisable to wear protective goggles for this stage.

10. Clean the textured area with methylated spirit. Paint on a traditional spray of flowers using a small pointer brush and iron red for the petals, yellow ochre and dark brown for the centres, and green for the leaves. Paint copper lustre over the textured area. Fire the brooch at 800°C (1475°F).

EMBEDDING JEWELS ~ *River design*

Before you begin, sketch out your ideas and try to develop patterns and images using nature and the world around you as a source of inspiration. You could take a simple shape such as a shell, flower or leaf, and then use colour to work out a harmonious design. The design on this page was inspired by an aerial view of a river.

Always work in the order shown below, and remember to start off with the technique that requires the highest firing, then reduce the temperatures for each subsequent firing.

YOU WILL NEED

Bone china trinket box

Chinagraph pencil

Groundlay oil

Pen oil

Powder paints: yellow and metallic gold

Lustres: brown and mother-of-pearl

Liquid bright gold

Relief enamel paste

Relief oil

Small scroller brush

Small pointer brush

Small square shader (synthetic)

Mapping pen

Small pieces of glass

Methylated spirit

Cotton bud

Small piece of sponge

Natural silk

Elastic band

Blender brush

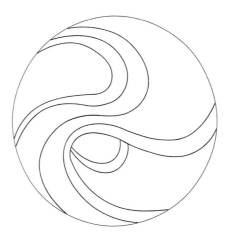

1. Use a chinagraph pencil to draw the design on to the surface of the trinket box.

2. Groundlay the metallic gold paint where required (see page 74). Fire at 780ºC (1435ºF). The chinagraph pencil lines will disappear when fired, so lightly mark the design lines back in using pen and yellow ink.

3. Mix relief enamel with relief oil to a stringy consistency and use a small scroller brush to drop in the raised lines as shown. Put a dot of paste on the underside of each piece of glass and press into place. Make sure all the relief work is complete and tidy. If necessary, clean the pieces of glass using a cotton bud dipped in methylated spirit. Fire at 770ºC (1420ºF).

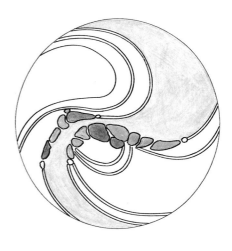

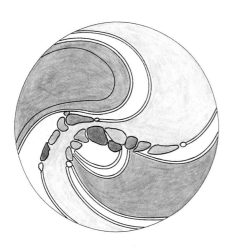

4. Use a small square shader to paint the brown areas shown here with brown lustre and use mother-of-pearl for the light sections. Fire at 740ºC (1365ºF).

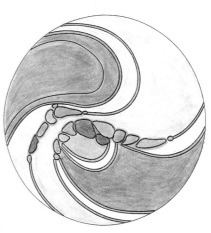

5. Use a small pointer brush to paint the decoration using liquid bright gold. Fire at 740ºC (1365ºF).

River design *The finished bone china trinket box*

Aerial view on bone china trinket box

This design was inspired by an aerial view of a motorway junction! The linear pattern was laid in with relief enamel, and thick areas were applied across the centre of the design. Blue glass was embedded in the paste. When dry, the box was fired at 780ºC (1435ºF). Some parts were painted with light blue lustre, and other areas were painted with mother-of-pearl lustre. The box was then fired at 760ºC (1400ºF). Platinum was painted on to the central band and around the stones. Extra fine platinum lines were added, and the box was fired at 760ºC (1400ºF).

Pearl and opal on bone china trinket box

Blue metallic paint was used as a groundlay and the box was fired at 780ºC (1435ºF). Relief enamel was shaped on the top of the box using a knife. Light and dark blue pieces of glass were then embedded in the paste. The box was fired at 780ºC (1435ºF). The relief enamel work was covered with platinum, carefully avoiding the pieces of glass. The box was fired at 760ºC (1400ºF). Finally, the pearl and opal were glued on to the lid.

Linear pattern on bone china trinket box

Gold base was painted on to the box. It was fired at 780ºC (1435ºF). A linear pattern was laid in with relief enamel using a small pointer brush. The brown glass was embedded in paste. When dry, the box was fired at 770ºC (1420ºF). It was then painted with liquid bright gold, working carefully around the brown glass. The box was fired at 760ºC (1400ºF).

Butterfly on bone china trinket box

For this piece, the box and the butterfly were purchased separately. Metallic silver was used as a groundlay on parts of the box and it was then fired at 780ºC (1435ºF). The butterfly and some areas of the box were painted with light blue lustre, other areas with mother-of-pearl lustre. The box and butterfly were then fired at 760ºC (1400ºF). A platinum linear pattern was painted on the box. The edges of the butterfly wings and the body were coloured with cobalt blue. The box and butterfly were fired at 760ºC (1400ºF). Finally, the butterfly was glued on to the lid.

Pansies on porcelain trinket box

Metallic gold paint was groundlaid over part of the box. It was then fired at 820ºC (1510ºF). A small pointer brush and relief paste were used to outline the flower petals and to paint in the stamens. The box was fired at 800ºC (1475ºF). Blue lustre was applied to the petals and the box was fired at 760ºC (1400ºF). The relief work was painted with gold and the box was then fired at 760ºC (1400ºF).

Floral design on porcelain trinket box
Flaking powder was applied around the design, and the box was fired at 820ºC (1510ºF). The glaze was chipped off and the surface cleaned with methylated spirit. The flower design was painted on to the lid and sides of the box, and it was then fired at 820ºC (1510ºF). The textured areas were painted with gold and the box was fired at 760ºC (1400ºF).

Winter scene on porcelain trinket box
Silver metallic paint was used as a groundlay to cover the box. It was fired at 820ºC (1510ºF). A small pointer brush was used to paint pale blue into the sky and blue-green into the water. The house, trees and bushes were painted using brown and touches of green. The box was fired at 810ºC (1490ºF).

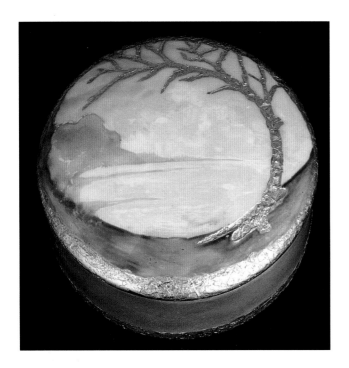

Landscape on porcelain trinket box
The design was drawn on and the flaking powder was applied to the tree and the edge of the lid. The box was fired at 820ºC (1510ºF). The flaked areas were chipped off and cleaned thoroughly with methylated spirit. Mother-of-pearl lustre was painted into the sky and water. Green was then laid in over the trees, foliage and landscape. Grey lustre was painted around the sides of the base. The box was fired at 760ºC (1400ºF). The textured areas were painted with platinum and the box was fired at 760ºC (1400ºF).

A. Tree and lake on porcelain brooch

Relief paste was laid in to depict the tree and rocks. Brown, green and blue glass chips were embedded in the paste. When dry, the brooch was fired at 820ºC (1510ºF). Blue lustre was painted into the sea, and yellow and green lustres into the horizon. Mother-of-pearl lustre was washed over the sky. The brooch was fired at 760ºC (1400ºF). The tree and areas around the glass were painted with gold. Two of the rocks and the leaves were painted with copper, and green lustre was painted in at the base of the rocks. The brooch was then fired at 760ºC (1400ºF).

B. Tree and sunset on porcelain brooch

Flaking powder was worked around the edge of the brooch, and over the tree trunk and branches. The brooch was fired at 820ºC (1510ºF). Glaze was chipped away from the trees and the border, and the area was then cleaned with methylated spirit. Yellow and green lustres were painted into the distance, and mother-of-pearl lustre was worked into the sky and lake. A grey lustre shadow was laid in behind the trees. The brooch was fired at 760ºC (1400ºF). The textured areas were painted with gold, and the leaves with copper. The brooch was fired at 760ºC (1400ºF).

C. Stormy tree on porcelain brooch

Flaking powder was applied to the central branch. When dry, the brooch was fired at 820ºC (1510ºF). The glaze was then chipped away from the branch, and the area cleaned with methylated spirit. Relief paste was applied to the remaining branches, and pieces of blue and green glass were firmly embedded. The brooch was fired at 800ºC (1475ºF). The background was then covered with mother-of-pearl lustre. When dry, the brooch was fired at 760ºC (1400ºF). Gold was painted on to the textured area and the relief branch. The brooch was fired at 760ºC (1400ºF).

D. Selection of porcelain brooches

Pieces of glass and enamel were embedded in relief paste and the brooches were fired at 800ºC (1475ºF). Lustres were painted on the background and the brooches were then fired at 760ºC (1400ºF). Gold and platinum lines were painted on, and the brooches were fired at 760ºC (1400ºF) Finally, the pearls were glued in place.

Orchids on porcelain plate
Flaking powder was used at the right of the design, and the plate was fired at 820ºC (1510ºF). The glaze was chipped away and the area cleaned well with methylated spirit. The orchids and background were painted using pink, yellow, blue, mauve and light green. The plate was fired at 820ºC (1510ºF). The shades were deepened to add tone and the plate was fired at 810ºC (1490ºF). Platinum was applied to the textured area. The plate was fired at 770ºC (1420ºF).

Butterfly on large, round porcelain tile
The design was drawn on using a chinagraph pencil and flaking powder was applied around the edge of the design, between the leaves. The tile was fired at 820ºC (1510ºF). The flaked areas were chipped away, and the surface cleaned with methylated spirit. The centre of the design was painted, and the tile was fired at 820ºC (1510ºF). Liquid bright gold was painted over the leaves and the textured background. The tile was fired at 770ºC (1435ºF). Greens and light browns were painted into the leaves, allowing the gold to peep through. A wipe-out tool was used to mark out the veins. A little dark penwork was added around the leaves. The tile was fired at 770ºC (1435ºF). A coat of platinum was added to the textured area and the tile was fired at 760ºC (1420ºF).

FROM LEFT TO RIGHT

Marbled porcelain vase

I-relief was laid around the top edge with a knife, and tiny coloured glass chips were embedded in the surface. The lower edge was groundlaid with copper metallic paint and the vase was fired at 820°C (1510°F). Dark brown and orange lustres were painted on and, when dry, marbling liquid was worked over the colours. The vase was fired at 760°C (1400°F). A gold line was painted in across the vase, and gold was applied to the area in relief. The vase was fired at 760°C (1400°F).

Gilded tree on porcelain vase

Flaking powder was applied to the top and bottom edges of the design, and to the tree trunk. The vase was fired at 820°C (1510°F). The glaze was chipped off, and the surface cleaned with methylated spirit. The background was painted with ivory, which was mixed using white, yellow and a tiny touch of pink. The vase was fired at 820°C (1510°F). I-relief was applied to the branches and the vase was fired at 800°C (1475°F). Liquid bright gold was applied to the design before the final firing at 760°C (1400°F).

Japanese design on porcelain vase

The design was sketched lightly on to the vase with a chinagraph pencil, then the cranes, lake and tree were outlined with a fine pen and black ink. Flaking powder was applied to the lake. When dry, the vase was fired at 820°C (1510°F). The glaze was chipped from the lake, and the area cleaned well with methylated spirit. The sky was painted with iron red, then sponged. The birds and the plum blossom were wiped out. Black was used to colour the tree, the cranes' beaks and their tail feathers. Ivory was painted over the land around the lake. A wipe-out tool was used to remove tiny lines from the far distance. The vase was fired at 820°C (1510°F). The plum blossom, the cranes' heads and the contour lines were coloured with gold. Platinum was laid in over the lake. The vase was fired at 770°C (1420°F).

Waves and butterflies on porcelain vase
The vase and the two butterflies were bought separately. The design was lightly drawn on to the vase with a chinagraph pencil. Metallic silver was groundlaid, and flaking powder was applied. The vase was fired at 820ºC (1510ºF). The flaked areas were chipped off and the area was thoroughly cleaned with methylated spirit. A small scroller brush was used to apply fine lines of enamel paste. The vase was fired at 800ºC (1475ºF). Lines of liquid bright gold were painted on and fine platinum lines were used over the relief work. Larger platinum bands were applied to the textured areas and the vase was fired at 760ºC (1400ºF). Pale blue raised paste dots were added to some of the platinum work, and some areas were coloured with blue lustre. The porcelain butterflies were painted with blue lustre and both the butterflies and the vase were fired at 760ºC (1400ºF). The butterflies were attached to the vase using strong glue.

Birds on an earthenware tile
Tiny drops of brown, orange, green, lilac and blue lustres were dropped on to the tile. Larger drops of lustre thinner were added, and swirled around in areas. The tile was fired at 760ºC (1400ºF). Some of the green lustre turned pink after this firing which gave a warm glow. Very dark green penwork was added to form the tree trunks and rocks. The tile was fired at 760ºC (1400ºF). White relief enamel birds were painted over the design. The tile was fired at 750ºC (1380ºF)

Butterflies on an earthenware tile
Tiny drops of light blue, green, lilac and light brown lustres were mixed separately with lustre thinner in a spoon and then dropped on to the tile. The colours were swirled around and dried with a hairdryer to create ripples. The tile was fired at 760ºC (1400ºF) The blue relief enamel butterflies were painted on. The tile was fired at 750ºC (1380ºF). A gold design was added around the edge of the tile following the shapes formed by the ripples around the edge and the butterflies were outlined using lines and dots. The tile was fired at 750ºC (1380ºF).

INTERPRETING DESIGNS

The following designs can be used in conjunction with the modern techniques shown in this chapter, or you could invent your own. Designs can be inspired by many things, especially nature. Many of my patterns and designs have their original source in nature and the environment: lakes, dams, rivers, rocks, ice, hills, cliffs, trees, leaves, roads, birds and butterflies for example.

Once you have decided upon your design, you should decide on the materials you wish to use, and choose a suitable colour scheme to work to. Always bear in mind the order of working, and remember that porcelain and bone china often require different firing temperatures.

First firing

Flaked work (porcelain only): 820ºC (1510ºF)
Groundlay with ordinary or metallic paint (porcelain): 820ºC (1510ºF)
Groundlay with ordinary or metallic paint (bone china): 780ºC (1435ºF)
Groundlay with ordinary or metallic paint (earthenware): 800ºC (1475ºF)

Second firing

Relief work with I-relief or raised paste (porcelain): 810ºC (1490ºF)
Relief work with I-relief or raised paste (earthenware): 780ºC (1435ºF)
Relief work with relief enamel (bone china): 770ºC (1420ºF)
Relief work with relief enamel (earthenware): 770ºC (1420ºF)

Third firing

Lustre work (porcelain and bone china): 760ºC (1400ºF)
Lustre work (earthenware): 760ºC (1400ºF)

Fourth firing

Gold, platinum and copper work (porcelain, bone china and earthenware): 760ºC (1400ºF)

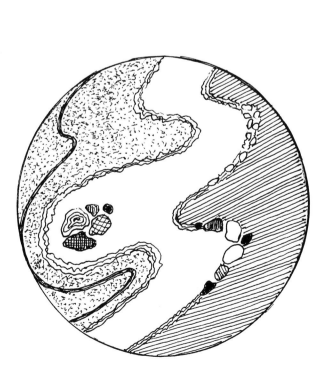

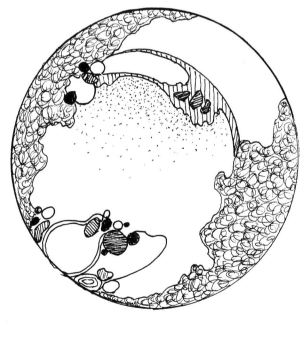

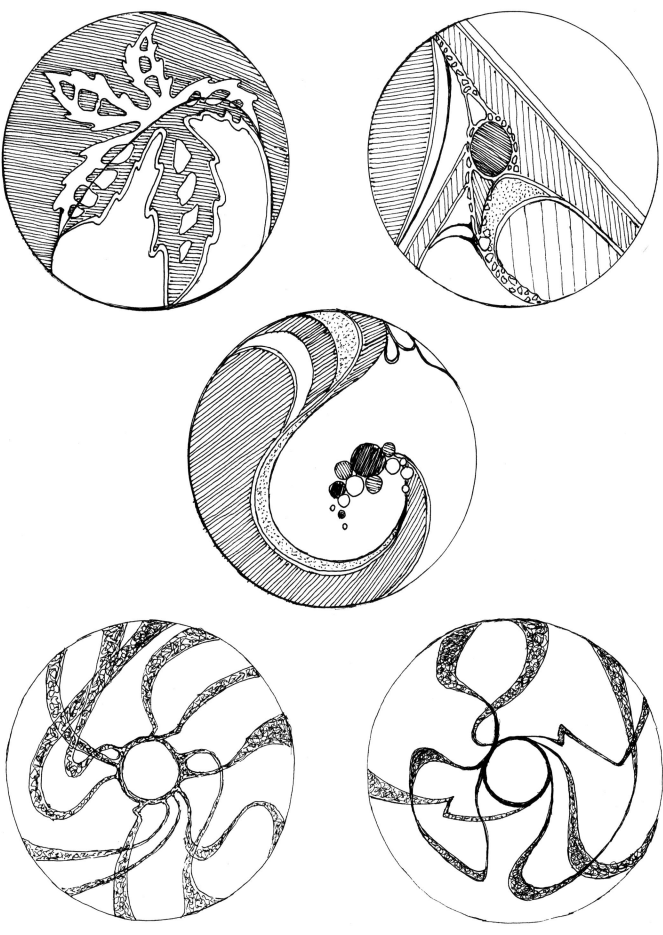

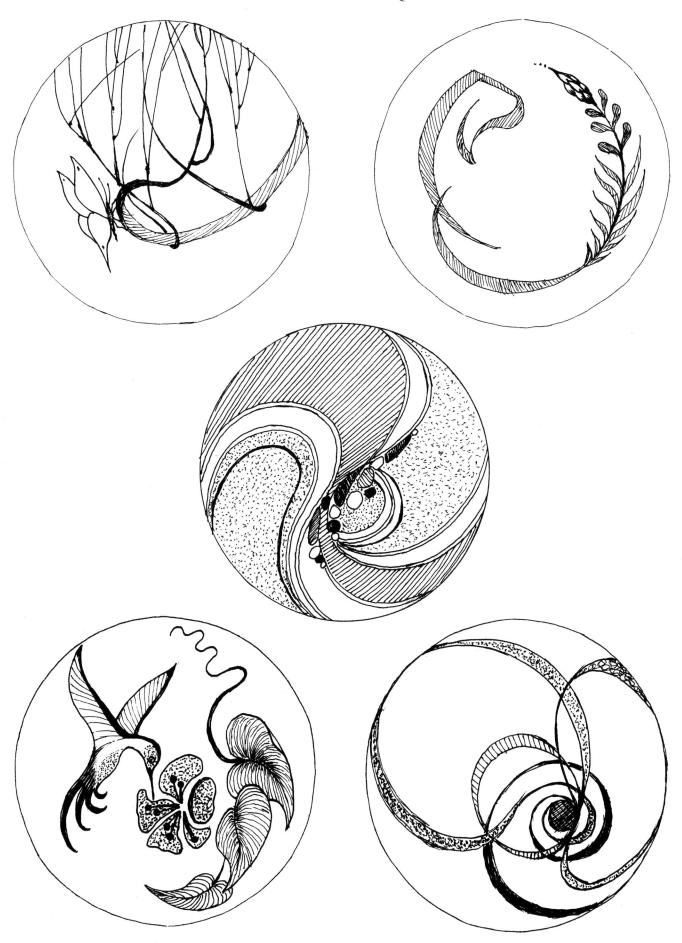

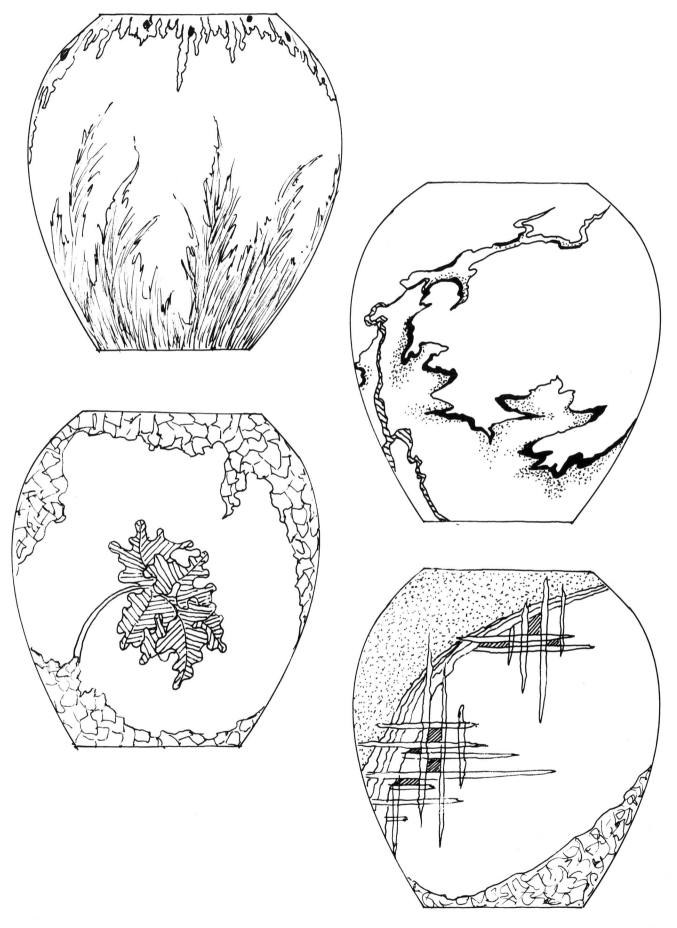

Kilns and firing

The simplest and cheapest way of firing is to find a specialist shop or local college that will fire your work for you or recommend someone who will do it. However, if you decide to purchase a kiln yourself, there are many types available. Some kilns are manufactured with the non-professional in mind, and these are relatively inexpensive and easy to use.

When purchasing a kiln, bear in mind its planned location and the amount of china painting you will be doing. I have a small electric kiln which can be used at home. It is loaded from the top and is most useful when firing small numbers of items. It is less expensive than the larger kilns, yet still wide enough to fire a 36cm (14in) dinner plate, and tall enough to fire a 30cm (12in) lamp base or vase. If you are buying a kiln, make sure it is sturdy and capable of firing to 1200ºC (2190ºF).

Firing fixes the colours, allowing you to build up successive layers and deepen the tones. These photographs show a coloured hibiscus tile after one firing at 800ºC (1475ºF), and after a second firing at 790ºC (1455ºF).

FIRING TEMPERATURES

Hot air rises, therefore the bottom of a larger kiln will be cooler than the top by a few degrees. One can lower the piece of china down the kiln for the second, third or fourth firing, so that the temperature for that piece is reduced each time. I keep a log of all the firings I do each year, then I have a record of temperatures and firing times (kilns fire quicker if not full, but it is wasteful and does not give such an even fire). The log also tells me how long the elements last. The temperatures shown right are intended to be used as a guide only.

Every kiln comes with a full set of instructions. Always read these thoroughly before firing. To fire your work, you should load it into a cold kiln. Set the kiln to the required temperature then leave it to heat up; the kiln will automatically switch itself off when it reaches the desired temperature. Leave your work in the kiln for at least ten hours to allow it to cool down gradually.

Porcelain
First firing: 820ºC (1510ºF)
Second firing: 820ºC (1510ºF)
Third firing: 810ºC (1490ºF)

Bone china
First firing: 780ºC (1435ºF)
Second firing: 780ºC (1435ºF)
Third firing: 770ºC (1420ºF)

Earthenware tiles
First firing: 800ºC (1475ºF)
Second firing: 790ºC (1455ºF)
Third firing: 790ºC (1455ºF)

LOADING THE KILN

You will need kiln furniture, such as stilts, cranks and batts (shelves), to stack and arrange painted pieces on and to make good use of the space available. Porcelain can be stacked without a problem – pieces can be positioned on top of one another with a small stilt between each plate. Bone china, however, needs careful handling as the glaze will melt and pieces can fuse pieces together if they are touching. These items need to be carefully separated, therefore fewer bone china pieces can be fitted into the kiln as each piece sits on a kiln batt.

THINGS THAT CAN GO WRONG

Do not worry if things go wrong during the firing process. It need not be a disaster.

- If you discover that your colours have faded or disappeared when you remove your items from the kiln, it means that they were fired at too high a temperature. Paint over the colours and re-fire at a lower temperature.
- If you discover that your colours are dull or matt and you can easily rub them off, the pieces have been fired at too low a temperature. Simply put them back in the kiln, and fire them at a higher temperature.
- If gold comes out with crack lines over it, it has been fired at too high a temperature. Rub it all out with a gold eraser. Apply it again and fire no higher than 760ºC (1400ºF).

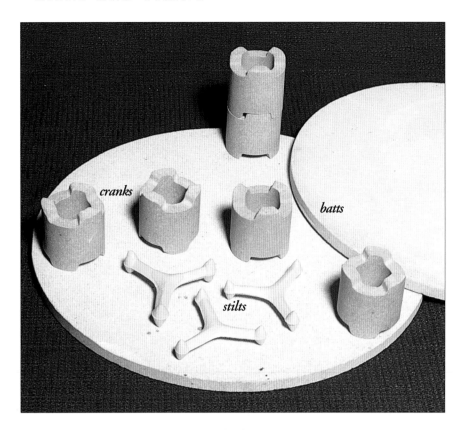

Kiln furniture showing batts, cranks and stilts

Loading the kiln with bone china

Loading the kiln with porcelain

NOTE

You can use batt wash to prevent items of china from sticking whilst in the kiln. Batt wash is a white powder that can be mixed with a little water to the consistency of milk. Paint it on to the batts of the kiln and tips of the stilts and allow to dry before china is positioned prior to firing.

Glossary

batt a shelf that fits in the kiln

batt wash powder that is mixed with water to prevent items sticking on the batt

bone china clay mixed with finely ground bone; it has a soft white glaze

burnishing gold a soft dull gold that is polished after firing using a burnishing pad, fibreglass brush or fine damp sand

chinagraph pencil a special pencil marker used to draw a design on to china. Also called a china marker.

earthenware coarse mixture of clay, available in white, cream or brick red

fat oil thickened pure turpentine used as a painting medium. It dries very quickly.

flaking powder used to remove the glaze from porcelain to create texture

gold base used as an undercoat for gold. It gives a matt finish.

gold eraser a very coarse eraser used to remove fired gold if a mistake has been made

lustre thinner used to thin lustres and bright liquid gold. This should be used very sparingly.

groundlaying a technique used to give an opaque finish to the china. Used to create a background.

groundlay oil used underneath powder paint for the groundlaying technique

I-relief relief powder suitable for use on porcelain, bone china and earthenware. It creates a raised surface.

kiln furnace used to fire china in and make the decoration permanent

kiln furniture the equipment that fits into the kiln and enables the china pieces to be stacked

lint-free cloth brushes are pressed on to lint-free cloth to remove surplus oil or paint

liquid bright gold shiny gold. It can be used straight from the bottle.

lustres shiny translucent colours, mostly precious metals in liquid form. They do not fuse with the glaze when fired but sit on the surface of the china.

mapping pen used to draw fine lines on china

marbling liquid this is dropped on to painted or lustred china to create a marbled effect

medium the oil used to mix the paints with, and to paint with

methylated spirit used to clean china with before it is painted

non-drying medium *see* open medium

on-glaze work the technique of painting on china

open medium a medium that does not dry quickly

palette box used to store mixed paints in

palette knife used to grind and mix paint

pâte sur pâte a technique of working in relief

peelable resist a liquid used to mask off areas of china

pen oil this is mixed with powder paint to produce an 'ink'

penwork the technique of drawing with a fine mapping pen

pipette a dropper used for oil, turpentine or water

porcelain china clay with a hard grey-white glaze

pure turpentine this is used to remove paint and to clean brushes. It is also used as a thinner for fat oil.

quick-drying medium a medium that dries quickly

raised paste a powder that is mixed with oil and used for relief work on porcelain and earthenware

relief enamel a powder that is mixed with oil and used for relief work on bone china and earthenware

reservoir pen a pen used with liquid bright gold to produce a fine line

running ground a technique of running turpentine through a surface that has been painted, before firing

silk square a piece of pure fine silk used to soften painted work. It is used over a small piece of sponge, and is held in place with an elastic band.

sugar water a mixture of icing sugar and water, used for penwork

wipe-out tool a rubber double-ended tool used to remove paint

**Convolvulus on an earthenware tile
by Pam Phillips**
*The flowers in this pen and wash painting were
outlined and painted simultaneously, instead of
the outline being drawn in first then fired, and
the colours added afterwards. The result was soft
and free, with no hard lines. Dark green
penwork was used on the leaves and they were
painted with light and dark green, with touches
of brown. Flowers were painted with a little
pink, blue and yellow. The tile was fired at
800ºC (1475ºF).*

Index